ON AND OFF PARNASSUS

Recent Publications by William Oxley:

ISCA   Exeter Moments (photography Barry Davidson),
(Ember Press, 2013)
Poems from the Divan of Hafez, trans. with Parvin Loloi,
(Acumen Publications 2013)
Collected and New Poems (Rockingham Press, 2014)
Walking Sequence & Other Poems
(Indigo Dreams Publishing, 2015)

William Oxley

On and off Parnassus

a book of Oxleydotes

Rockingham Press

Published in 2018 by
Rockingham Press
11 Musley Lane,
Ware, Herts SG12 7EN
www.rockinghampress.co.uk

British Library Cataloguing-in-Publication Data

A catalogue record for this book
is available from the British Library

ISBN 978-1-904851-72-1

Contents

1.   On and Off Parnassus   7
2.   Not your Average Christmas   12
3.   A Poet's Funeral   27
4.   The '59 Club   33
5.   Lost in Llandrindod   38
6.   A Yorkshire Lass   45
7.   Sleeping with John Heath-Stubbs   49
8.   The Safranière   54
9.   More about Tony   57
10.   Journey to Vienna   64
11.   A Birthday Treat   69
12.   Blackmailed into Fame   74
13.   The Unforgettable Torriano   86
14.   The Absentee Landlady   92
15.   Remembering Ken Smith   100
16.   Our Life is not our own   106
17.   Ostracism by Proxy   111
18.   Living Ghosts or the Art of Obituary   115
19.   The Chessman Cometh   121
20.   A Friend in Need   126
21.   Name-dropping   132
22.   The Ultimate Removal   135
23.   The Birthday Party   143
24.   The Living Dead   150
25.   Falling Asleep in the Palace   154
26.   Picking up the Pieces   157
27.   Afterword   172

Acknowledgements

Thanks to the following publications which first featured some of these chapters: *Acumen Literary Journal, The French Literary Review, Horizon on-line Magazine (Salt), Smiles Above the Platform (Marc Goldring Books), Stand Magazine* and *Torriano Nights (Acumen Publications).*

1.
ON AND OFF PARNASSUS

Art imitates life, or life imitates art...or whatever. In old-fashioned comedy shows especially, the ludicrous was a constant source of laughter. Why? Because scenes, however improbable-seeming in reality, did draw on life.

Many years ago, I was invited to give a reading of my poems at the Plough Arts Centre in Great Torrington, North Devon. I had never been there before, but I found the whole venture to be fascinating. First of all, I knew that as a user of public transport such as myself, and a dweller in South Devon, it would be necessary to take the romantically-named Tarka Line from Exeter to Barnstaple. This rail line is so named after Henry Williamson's famous book about Tarka the Otter which lived in the River Taw in North Devon. Also, it was the rare railway journey where passengers were required to tell the engine driver, via the guard, where to stop the train for them to alight at most intermediate non-stops before the terminus at Barnstaple.

So we had to tell the guard we wanted to alight at a place called Umberleigh. The train stopped seemingly in the middle of nowhere, as the saying is, with a small house – once the station master's office – its garden filled with cottage flowers but no other sign of habitation. Outside, and facing us, was a long steep hill down which we saw tearing an old banger at a seemingly impossible speed. This turned out to be our host for the weekend, who apologised for being late but who had been delayed with some final problems about the forthcoming festival .Likewise at the end of our stay we would be similarly conveyed to the same station where it seemed very odd to be standing on a platform waiting for a train to emerge from the tunnel and having to flag it down like a bus!

Thus were we conveyed to Torrington. On arriving, we discovered it to be a small town divided into two layers, of which Great Torrington the upper layer was perched on a steep hillside above the River Taw. Someone else met Patricia and I – I think it was the organizer of the arts festival then taking place – and conducted us to our billet for the day and night we were required to be there. The person whose hospitality we were to enjoy was a man in his early seventies called

Bill Joslin, a retired civil servant who, in that employment, had been the curator of the artworks in all the British embassies world-wide. Bill, as it turned out, now bore the title of 'Unofficial Mayor of Torrington', though we never discovered why, save that wandering the streets later everyone whom we encountered appeared to be an intimate acquaintance of Mr Joslin, virtually doffing their forelocks to him.

The evening of the poetry reading was also the evening of the annual Torrington Carnival; an event that attracted hundreds of people from Britain and abroad. It was a colourful and impressive event, the focal point of which was the town square. But as the square began to fill up uncomfortably, Bill said we needed a better view of the proceedings and marched us straight into a nearby house and upstairs where we shared the view of the carnival with the house owner and his family. Afterwards I asked Bill were the occupants of the house friends of his – they seemed to know him – but he replied 'Oh, no, of course not.' Because the poetry reading did not start till after the carnival was over, it became the latest poetry reading I ever gave, namely, 11.30pm at night... and I was not the last reader, who was the poet Elma Mitchell, whose reading spanned midnight.

Finally, two other things I recall. Firstly, that Patricia and I spent the night in one of the bedrooms of Bill Joslin's house. We slept in the bed, and when we arose the next morning another waking poet emerged from under the same bed. Secondly, at some point during our visit to this town – famously besieged during the English Civil War – we were taken out for a sumptuous meal by the Unofficial Mayor. Among our fellow guests at the restaurant was the Director of the Plough Arts Festival. And as if to emphasize what an exhausting business arts administration is, without any warning the Director fell forward asleep into his soup... something one normally witnessed only in film comedies or among the antics of circus clowns.

The world of poetry, besides producing poems, throws up the odd and the unexpected. This is because the imaginative life is different, if only in degree, from so-called 'real' life. Bradford, Yorkshire is a world away from Torrington. Indeed, to arrive in the twilight in Bradford nowadays, one's first impression is not that of the real or imaginative life there, but of the pervasive smell of curry. You could be in downtown Delhi, save that restaurants in Bradford are not protected outside by uniformed soldiers or persons carrying shotguns, as they often are in India. Once again, it was poetry that took us there: the reading of poems that is; and in Bradford's Central Library. Poetry readings in libraries are usually serious occasions, almost solemn. But this time the Muse, or someone, had decided it should be otherwise. The publisher for this reading tour in the North of England, leaned towards the lectern on the small stage to introduce the readers, and the lectern collapsed into a dozen pieces. No humour, in any of the poems subsequently read, drew a fraction of the laughter that this 'reverse art installation', as it might be called, produced.

In the so-called Poetry World, things seldom go badly wrong. But they do go wrong sufficiently to produce either the unfortunately memorable image or the full-blown anecdote. As an illustration of the former, which could have become the latter also, I was participating in a reading in St. Peter's College, Oxford. One of the readers was the poet Jane Kirwan, who is also a part-time dentist in North London but lives, for some of each year with her Czech partner in Prague. She entered the college reading room with her face covered in blood. Unfortunately, she had walked into a completely glass door that was so clean she had not been aware it was a door.

I may be the only poet in Britain to have been thumped in the chest by a drunken Poet Laureate. Whom I will not name, if only for my own safety! In discussion with the said laureate at a London party, I made the observation that 'I didna ken you wes Scottish?' I spoke in my best imitation Scots' accent, transforming myself into a stage Scotsman for a laureate whose accent was not remotely Scottish. My only reward being the aforesaid 'thumping'. Though I must add that, having just discovered the laureate's Scottish connection, I also was somewhat inebriated.

A poet only truly feels he or she is 'on Parnassus' on a few occasions. Or, rather, on all single occasions when a poem arrives to be made in what used to be called – in the days before workshops and creative writing courses – 'moments of inspiration'. In the Nineties Patricia and I used to stay at the Abses' house in Golders Green, often when Dannie and Joan were away in Wales. This was because we are quite used to cats, and the Abses had a cat. Dannie being the best-known Welsh poet since Dylan Thomas, they had named their cat

'Caitlin' after Dylan's wife. The guest bedroom in the Abses' house was a single, large attic room converted. But, occasionally, when there was a strong wind about, the attic room was not the best room to sleep in because of noise. On the 22nd October 1994 at 4am (it said so in my notebook) I was seated at the white kitchen table: a wind-induced insomniac. Drinking a cup of tea (or something stronger), I was musing quietly to myself, Patricia asleep two floors above me, when suddenly a poem came to me and I scribbled it down in my notebook. I knew straight away, on reading it back to myself, that it was a poem which needed almost no revision; and that it was as good a suburban poem as I would ever write. Indeed, I liked it a lot more than most poems I write: I had confidence in it, and in that others would like it too. It was a poem that led to a somewhat strange experience. A year or two later, I was notified by a journal in the City of Bath that ran a quarterly poetry competition, that a poem of mine had been given a 'highly commended' in the shortlist of one of its competitions. So I looked it up in the magazine which subsequently printed the winner and runners-up of the competition. Now, my poem was entitled 'The White Table', its locus of inspiration. But there was no poem by that name, but there was one called 'Tabula Rasa', and it was followed by the lines and stanzas of my poem. I ascribed the change of title to the adjudicator feeling he (I knew it was a he) could improve it with a different title (he may have been drunk at the time for all I knew). But stranger still was the fact that 'The White Table' had not, at that time, been published anywhere... nor had I entered it in this competition. Very odd.

Poets have an odd, even dangerous reputation to most people. After all, it was the writing of a poem (obliquely about Stalin) that cost Osip Mandelstam his life. I was once invited to write a poem to celebrate the wedding of a young couple and to read the poem at the reception. The reception, following the wedding at a church in Oxfordshire, was in the sumptuous surroundings of Blenheim Palace. At the end of the meal, I was to read the poem to all the guests. Well, just as the coffee and *digestifs* had been delivered, I was approached by the head waitress. Said she to me: 'Are you the poet?' 'Er, yes...' I answered somewhat diffidently. In accusatory tone she continued: 'You have written a poem which you are to read soon?' Me: 'That's correct.' 'Well, I hope you don't mind me asking, but is there anything in the poem likely to offend the other guests?' 'Er... what sort of offensive things?' 'Well, religious, political, sexual things...?' said She. 'No, I don't think so.' I replied.

'Good!' she exclaimed and walked away. The following day, at breakfast, I told this little anecdote to the husband and wife who had organized the wedding reception for their son and his bride. The wife was 'utterly appalled', but the husband just laughed.

TS Eliot wrote of the 'impersonality of all great art', and a close reading of, say, the plays of Shakespeare (despite the Sonnets), or of Sophocles, would seem to preclude the personal, autobiographical element. In fact, it was probably William Wordsworth in 'The Prelude' who first raised the question of making poetry out of the poet's own life story. 'The Prelude' is a mixture of life story and soliloquy of thoughts: philosophising upon the poet's self. The debate between Wordsworth and Coleridge at the time of the making of *The Lyrical Ballads* is perhaps germane here. For Coleridge regarded 'the Truth' as divinely given and did not approve of the delivering of truth 'through other men's mouths'. Which, of course, is what playwrights do. But, at other times, he seemed to approve of 'ventriloquizing the Truth'. In more recent times the post-WW2 'Confessional Poets' like Plath, Sexton, Robert Lowell, *et al*, seemed to definitely approve the practice of making poems out of one's own life and experience. With the result that the majority of poems today, when they are not simple descriptions of the visible world (and do not rise above mere description), are distinctly autobiographical. And I do not exempt my work from the latter: except that I try, when writing what are called 'poems of place', to evoke the genius loci, ignoring as far as possible my own presence in the place. I cannot, of course, claim always to be successful in that intention, if only for the fact of poetry and poetic thought being different: as, in philosophical thought, between subject and object. Consequently, there is something then for a poet between being on Parnassus and being off Parnassus. And while on Parnassus gives us poems, off Parnassus gives us anecdotes, but which will never provide the depth of illumination that the good poem provides. And I offer as answer to the question 'What use is poetry?' that it 'adds an imaginative dimension to life'. As for philosophy, well, that is another matter. In *The Republic* Plato said 'All poets are liars'. I once wrote a book of philosophy that a Hampstead bookseller said was 'Too intellectual for Hampstead'. The Hampstead that is reckoned to be the Intellectual Capital of Great Britain! That was reported to me by a book sales person, so it is not a lie. So there is obviously an anecdotal side to more writing than just poetry.

2.
NOT YOUR AVERAGE CHRISTMAS

Bearing no ill-will to the various world religions – without necessarily agreeing with all their tenets – I am sometimes asked to explain what appears, to many people, an intolerable benevolence on my part. My answer is simple: I am rather more inclined to direct my negative feelings towards the men and women who have perverted religious teachings and beliefs, rather than towards the religions themselves. For this reason I have been usually happy to celebrate Christmas, though I am in no senses anything more than an idle, backslid, non-practising, non-communion-taking, unbaptised Christian. Which is to say, something like an English agnostic, though one rather inclined to endorse much of Christ's teaching. – But, anyway, that's enough of that. All I really want to say is that Christmas festivities and myself get on quite well.

Not always too easy though were the years Patricia and I cared for two mothers and two daughters mostly under the same roof. Tricky you might think? You'd be right. But there was nothing I could do about it, as I had brought it on myself without even thinking about it. Nor did I have any idea how long the Caring Years would last. The reason being, of course, that poets have no more foresight than anyone else – as Dannie Abse ruefully relates after meeting his then local MP in the 1960s, Margaret Thatcher, and telling his wife afterwards, 'That woman will never get anywhere in politics.'

Now, the point of this domestic information is to try to account for the fact (as it does, I suspect) that as long as we had two mothers to care for, and the children, Patricia and I never had a Christmas away from home. We were never restless about this. What is more, my gifted wife created wonderful Christmases at home. Excellent social occasions. Beautiful times. Even when my mother and mother-in-law were both dead, and the kids had gone off wedded, so that Patricia and I were alone, it did not occur to us we might spend Christmas occasionally away from home. Then enter James Brockway. An ex-civil servant who had served as a bomb-aimer in the war against Japan. Voluntarily exiled to the Netherlands, James became a distinguished translator of Dutch literary works into English and vice versa. A man who had, so to speak, fled this country in the early Fifties to dwell in more liberal Holland, having first discovered himself homosexual then, more awkwardly still, a poet – two powerful blows to his sense of security.

Sometime in the late 1980s he began sending translations of modern Dutch poets to Patricia for her magazine *Acumen*. Like many homosexuals James seemed more at ease, less threatened by women. He numbered among his pen pals and 'chums' such celebrities as the film star Joan Crawford and the novelist Iris Murdoch. Eventually, he turned up on our doorstep, bringing his birdlike figure, and the personality sealed within it, to delight us. Occasionally, too, we would meet him in the Metropolis.

James was a fine translator of Dutch poets like Rutger Kopland, Marc Tritsmans, Patty Scholten and others. Patty Scholten's delightful animal poems had their first magazine publication in the UK in *Acumen*. As for his own poetry, it was particularly concerned with universals like time and nature; he was a fine craftsman who tried never to release a poem prematurely. From time to time we exchanged poems for opinion and suggested corrections. The quality of his work was recognized by both *Acumen* and *The London Magazine*: and both Enitharmon Press and Rockingham Press brought out collections in the UK. While in the Netherlands he translated prose works by the likes of Iris Murdoch and Muriel Spark into Dutch; and he introduced to Britain a number of Dutch prose writers. In his lifetime in the Netherlands he was knighted by the Dutch Government for his services to literature; and some years after his death a major literary award was introduced in memory of him.

This diminutive but ebullient man claimed he was wealthy but not entirely healthy, suffering as he undoubtedly did from angina, which was kept under control by tablets. A man who would, when alone, sing to himself like a songbird; in company, whether of his familiars or not, he was highly and amusingly sociable. But, like many older folk, he was unpredictable.

Between our house in The Mount and Churston Ferrers village is a path that meanders beside some woods and bisects a wide, oval field. As the three of us approached this field one day, Sir Jim (as he liked to be called from time to time) suddenly said, 'Where am I?' As the three of us continued along the path, Patricia and I sought to pull him back to earth, stop his mind wandering. This was not an unfamiliar walk to him, so his abrupt insistence that we were 'walking along a dried-up river bed' was absurd – absurd and disconcerting. Then, as the path traversed the oval field – a huge clearing skirted by trees – James insisted, 'I must lie down.' So, skipping away from the path at a right angle, he prostrated himself in the weed and stubble. We rushed to his side. 'I must have a sugar sandwich!' he cried. James was a diabetic. He made us search his pockets for a pink tablet (for angina), and he placed it underneath his tongue. Stretched out full length at about twenty feet to one side of the path, with his eyes fast shut, and Patricia seated by his head and me at his feet, the scene must have looked like a Red Indian burial ceremony when two women came by walking their dogs. Certainly they looked curiously at us. Then it began to rain. We said to our companion, 'You can't have a sugar sandwich here, James. Either we go on to the Churston Court Hotel, or we go back the way we've come?'

We went back: half-carrying the little old man; half frogmarching him. To get back home we had to pass the Fishcombe Holiday Camp. In the bar there – it being open to non-residents – we obtained a sugar-filled sandwich for 'Sir' Jim. It helped restore him somewhat. After a bit, we called up a taxi to take us up the short but steep hill back to The Mount. As James informed us he had gone very cold despite the sunshine, we immured him in our conservatory with a shawl over his knees. In the conservatory the temperature soars at the least appearance of sun. Our guest fell asleep for three or more hours. While we – who had thought he was going to die on us – had a strong drink each.

Later, when he was fully *compos mentis* again, James apologized for scaring us, before blaming the whole thing on us for 'treating him too well' with our hospitality (including wine). 'You see,' he sighed, 'I don't get many English visitors in Den Haag, apart from Alan Ross, and he seldom comes now. When I do I get very excited. But nobody comes now, not even at Christmas.' This not being the first time he had spoken in this self-pitying tone, I burst out in a sudden fit of compassionate irritation, 'Alright, James, we'll come!' Now that Patricia's mother, had died in the February of that year, as had my mother a few years earlier, it seemed a good idea to have our first Christmas away from home for more than a quarter of a century. But how wrong we were! Or right if we had been seeking a truly *memorable* Christmas.

That Christmas Eve we took the Eurostar train to Brussels, having first purchased a bottle of ready-opened red wine to aid us on our sub-Channel passage lasting approximately half an hour – something we had not experienced before. There was the usual talk of claustrophobia from Patricia. It was, however, a straightforward journey. At least it was until we arrived on the platform (number forgotten, but it could have been 9) at Brussels' Station. The platform from which our train was due to depart at 21.15 hours (that I do recall) to The Hague. It was up there on the indicator board. Unfortunately, a few minutes later the entire Departures' board went completely blank as if there had been a power cut.

On the platform there were, perhaps, two hundred or more passengers: among them several recognizable couples who had shared our carriage on the train from London's Waterloo Station. The first two nearest us were fairly nondescript but polite students; one male, one female. The female was English, her fair hair draped over her rucksack strapped to her back. The other was a Dutch youth of about 19 years who had closely-shaven hair and a helpful manner. Words in Belgian-French were suddenly blasted out by the loudspeaker system. Though Dutch, the young man was a linguist and could interpret for the rest of us. He informed us that the Belgian railways (it being Christmas Eve) had decided to go on strike. Stranding us and, doubtless, thousands of others all over Belgium.

It is at such moments, and in such circumstances, that the English decide it is perhaps time they talked to each other – even foreigners, provided the latter speak English. Despite being a mongrel nation whose country is multiracial (the term that has now replaced the far more civilized 'cosmopolitan'), we still seem incapable of becoming multilingual. But, be that as it may, the little group which we formed in that moment of instant *camaraderie* – and on the solid foundation that we had noticed each other on the under-Channel express – consisted of the two students already described; ourselves, a very pretty Persian-looking girl who resembled the daughter of an Anglo-Persian family of our acquaintance; and two others. The latter were the most memorable stars in this small, instant galaxy: a large black woman called Melrose and her son, whose name we did not at first catch.

Melrose, like her name, was wonderful. She was an outward going, merry dame of West Indian extraction: a New Briton, Brixton born and bred. Her presence and personality were expansive as a black umbrella in the rain; though she was all sun. A handsome woman not discreetly attired, unlike her timid-seeming son, she was successfully hiding the fact that she was forty – or even a bit more. Hers was a loud but not unpleasant personality. She embodied fun, and had a quick-witted mind with a voice that boomed London Town. She seemed to easily embarrass her offspring.

I took to her immediately. I have to confess I got on very well with Melrose throughout this little emergency. After some talk among ourselves, we decided on a plan of virtual inaction – i.e. we'd leave Platform 9 (or whatever its number was) and go in search of the Information Office. Descending from the platform along with many others with the same idea, we reached a sort of long stone corridor linking all the station platforms, and were in good time to hear an incomprehensible but heated argument between a passenger at the head of a queue in front of the booking office window and the official behind the glass. Abruptly the window was shut in the passenger's face – in all our faces – and that seemed that.

It was at that point I had my moment of inspired demagoguery. I leapt up on a wooden bench in the concourse, like Lenin addressing a revolutionary crowd, and started a rant which began, 'This is the first time I have ever set foot on Belgian soil, and... 'I paused to gain effect, then bawled, 'And it will be the last! For this disgraceful strike – called without warning – is a blasphemy against the whole spirit of the European Community, a blasphemy against Christmas (and therefore against God), and a deliberate attack against the ordinary citizen designed to cause the maximum suffering. The separation of families and friends deliberately done is an act of malevolence against the people! So if the railway workers are on strike, and the station staff will not deal with us, I say we should take direct action...'

'Like what?' demanded a voice.

'Like... like picking up these benches and using them as battering rams to break into the ticket office or information centre or the station master's office... or any office where we will get a hearing.' I didn't notice till later all benches were bolted firmly to the floor

'Get down off your platform, Mr Poet!' yelled Melrose hooting with laughter and adding, 'You look ridiculous.'

So I did… get down.

Fortunately, no more speechmaking or threats of direct action from me were necessary. A uniformed station official arrived and addressed us in both French and English. What he said was, 'Zere is a train for Rotterdam soon. From zere you weel be able to get a connection to ze Hague and Amsterdam.' To which Melrose said noisily and crossly, 'Fuckin' Rotterdam!' – thus displaying the direct, plain-speaking side of her character for the first time. And, as if to provide greater interpretation of her gnomic apostrophe, she turned to her son and added, 'We don't fuckin' want to go to fuckin' Rotterdam, do we Cynthia?' Or at least that is what her young companion's name sounded like. But the figure shrank more and more into its outsize anorak.

It was not until our little group of Brits was settled in a carriage of the putative Rotterdam train, that the reason for the application of the nomenclature 'Cynthia' to the somewhat masculine figure became apparent. When proper introductions had been made all round, everyone realized that Melrose's shy and retiring son was, in fact, a daughter. Modern gear on young or old can be most confusing at times.

By now we were all getting on famously; and the journey was beginning to become less of a nightmare for everyone save Melrose's offspring. The latter, like a tortoise, was forever shrinking into a shell with each utterance of her mother. The rest of us talked convivially, getting to know each other better and better. Melrose had learned I was a poet by eavesdropping on Patricia's and my conversations on the Eurostar express. The Persian-looking girl told us she was going like us to spend her Christmas in Den Haag, only with her father who was separated from her mother. The two students were going to have their Christmas vacation with one set of their parents – his. But, once more, Melrose proved the most memorable in her reason for undertaking this journey in the festive season. After telling us – claiming – she was a lawyer in chambers in the Inns of Court, she confessed, 'But I'm off to Amsterdam to spend the vacation working as a hooker.'

Everyone was dumbfounded to think of this elegant and vivacious black lady lawyer (if that's what she was) spending Christmas plying an older, and even more disreputable trade than the law, to earn some extra money. I couldn't help bursting out laughing; but none of us could really form an adequate response to Melrose's extraordinary claim. All Patricia and I could tell the black woman was that we were going to spend a quiet Christmas with an old poet in The Hague (Den Haag in Dutch). A predictable and dull Christmas once we could get there, we thought.

Before, however, we could discuss the joys of prostitution further, the train pulled up in a big station. Not Rotterdam but Antwerp: a gothic cathedral of a place and a dead end station as well. As this fact was gradually born in on all passengers, a small man with a somewhat ratlike demeanour, ran through our carriage shouting 'Vive la France!' and punching the air with his fists. We deduced he was French, and followed him off the train, before losing sight of him. We were carried along in a tide of disgruntled passengers to find ourselves eventually in a vast and ornate booking hall. It was packed with hundreds of passengers starting, once again, to form into national groupings like voluntarily penned sheep.

Suddenly, we spotted the tiny Frenchman again; and also TV cameras. The small man was beside himself with rage and engaged in kicking and punching the biggest station porter I have ever seen. The TV people were busily filming the fight, and I knew that our Christmas Eve crisis had entered its media stage. At the same moment too I discovered that our coloured and colourful companion Melrose was truly English, when she grabbed my arm to hold me back from going across to get a better view of the fight scene, 'Don' get involved, Mr Poet!'

After the near-rioting and posturing for the Media had subsided, a gendarme frogmarched the diminutive Frenchman away, and everyone else was gradually shepherded outside of the main entrance to Antwerp Station. There to await the coming of buses which were intended to transport us through the night to a station on the Dutch border called Roosendaal. In the scrimmage which ensued to board the long, bendy buses, our group lost the two young students and nearly got separated from the beautiful Persian girl called Yasmin. Finally, though, we were on our way – or hoped we were. As it was, by then, getting towards midnight, and Melrose had some wine left, we decided to celebrate.

The bus rushed its way through the black Belgian countryside which seemed all roads locked into a landscape of shadowy trees. Alas, only our little group of foolish Britons was jolly and talkative – our fellow passengers who were Dutch, German, Belgian and French were very subdued. This is how that late night dialogue went:

Melrose: 'Cheers!'

Them: silence.

Melrose: 'Fuck you then!'

We drank the last of the wine. Then Melrose again, 'Anybody got any food?'

Yasmin: 'I have this.' Digs box out of luggage.

Melrose: 'I bloody hate Turkish Delight!'

Me: 'Well, I love it.'

The rest of us accepted pieces of the Turkish Delight and began consuming them with pleasure.

Melrose (shrugging): ''Suppose I'd better have some too.'

Cynthia: 'Oh, mother!' (for umpteenth time).

About half the box had been eaten when the bus suddenly came to a halt.

Melrose: 'Why we stopped?'

No one knew. So Melrose craned her neck to see out of the window, Patricia: 'I think the driver's got out?'

Melrose (shrieking): 'Jesus, he has! He's legged it. Abandoned us. What we do now?'

German (nearby seat); 'Nein. Iss going to read der signs.'

Melrose: 'Wotseesay? Signs... wot signs?'

Yasmin: 'In Belgium they have maps at the roadside to help when you are lost.'

Melrose: 'Jesus! Are we lost?'

Yasmin: 'Probably.'

German: 'Ja, he iss lost.'

Melrose: 'That's all we fuckin' need!'

A silence then descended on the bus; broken only by the German nearest us who kept saying half-aloud to himself, 'Ja, I can drive a bus. Ja, I can.' But none of us showed any enthusiasm for the fact, nor were comforted by it. Eventually, however, the driver returned and, once more, took his bus thundering through the utterly moonless and starless night.

It was nearly one in the morning when we reached Roosendaal. We should have been tucked up in bed an hour ago at Sir Jim's apartment. The station consisted of a cavernous booking hall built in Thirties' style, plus two very long platforms – one 'up' and one 'down', as they say. The booking hall was choked with an array of weary passengers, many stretched out on the concrete floor. They ranged from respectable Dutch burghers to obvious drunks and junkies of varying nationalities. One of the latter, a giant with blond hair and lager can in his hand, came and seated himself next to me the moment we boarded the train for Den Haag and Amsterdam. He had a scruffy dog with him, and both stank to high heaven. He tried to interrogate me for some time but his English was poor. Eventually he gave up and moved elsewhere. Melrose and Cynthia, Yasmin and Patricia almost immediately fell asleep.

After only one or two more minor snags, one involving our arrival at the wrong station in The Hague, the other the kind gift of a coin by Yasmin that enabled us to use the telephone (we had only paper money), we finally arrived at James's apartment in the Riouwstraat, some four and a half hours late. James's apartment, consisting of two distinct parts separated by a central hallway, with the telephone there cut off from either part by glass doors, he greeted us with, 'If I hadn't got up to answer a call of nature, I'd never have heard the 'phone ring. You were saved by my weak bladder!' He gave one of his tootling little laughs – almost, but not quite, a giggle.

Over the years – especially when travelling – I have noticed how Patricia and I have been frequently 'saved' by the littlest of things: things which so easily could have gone against us but didn't. Fate or what?

James gave us hot soup and rolls, and me an excellent bottle of claret, before we were put to bed in the guest room. In a wooden-sided bed, exactly like a double coffin with heavy carvings on it. Besides being a writer, James Brockway was an aesthete.

On Christmas morning – after a breakfast that was half-English, half-Continental – we were taken to meet an Anglo-Dutch family who were his friends. It was a miserable, cold grey day with mist draped between the trees, and it was only the interest of an unfamiliar environment that kept our spirits up. We were not invited to the

Christmas lunch at James's friends' place; but were welcomed and given sherry and mince pies. A pleasant but uneventful visit to a house of modest artistic refinement – modern where James's apartment was more in the Edwardian decorative style. Where James had genuine Renaissance figurines and Salvatore Rosa and Romney paintings, his 'chums' (always a word of his) had Mondrian and Van Gogh prints on pale cream walls, with tubular steel chairs with fat pastel-coloured cushions.

Back at James's flat, we were given a lunch of jugged hare, prepared for him in advance by 'My plumber.' He said, 'He and I talked over what you might like for today, and he was sure you would welcome a change from turkey, hence the jugged hare. Roland – that's his name – is a good cook.' Then James added, 'After Bron died, Roland used to come round every Thursday for sex. He couldn't come at weekends – he has a wife.' Bron was his partner for many years.

Thoughtfully we ate our jugged hare and began to feel relaxed after the trauma of our nearly-overnight journey. James had all kinds of things in his cocktail cabinet; but sherry, gin and wine were what we mainly drank. As we were drowsy after the meal, our host insisted we watched his favourite film starring his favourite actress – Greta Garbo: I think it was – called *Grand Hotel.* I thought little of it; but James knew every line of its dialogue, and eagerly anticipated each scene like a child being reread a familiar book. There was something childlike in James and one didn't want to say anything critical or cynical to him. Besides, he was, as I say, our kindly host.

The next day, Boxing Day, Sir Jim got his motor car along from wherever he kept it garaged, and drove us to the North Sea resort of Scheveningen. What had once been, according to James, the fashionable Deauville of The Netherlands, was now a sort of 'hideously built-up Manhattan-by-Sea', as I described it in a letter to my daughter Elizabeth. The North Sea was calmly grey and befogged; the immensely long beach was a yellow shale of small pebbles; and crowds were walking up and down the promenade. It was a day of white faces and red noses because of the raw temperature outside.

After taking morning coffee in a leather-seated café with indifferent waitresses and fruit machines, James drove us back to the Riouwstraat. He was very enthusiastic about everything to do with poetry and place;

and though he lamented the 'modernizing' of Scheveningen, he had viewed the resort with a mixture of affection and nostalgia for what it had been like when he, and his long-term partner, the late Bron, had first known it. He was excitable and full of life, and said we were 'bad for his old heart' but was nevertheless glad we had 'come for Christmas'.

Next, despite the deepening cold outside, he was determined to take us to see the Dutch Parliament buildings. 'A sight not to be missed!' he insisted. From a wide square lined with winter's leafless trees we gazed across a waterway at the impressive pile. Less in height but as seemingly extensive as Westminster, and certainly bigger than the Elysée Palace in Paris. The sky above held abundant promise of snow, but it was far too cold for a flake to fall.

At first, it seemed that everywhere James knew for lunching was shut this Boxing Day. But, then, in a narrow street just off the parliament square, we discovered a small, cosy-looking bistro and went in. It was a place of only a few tables with a bar at one end. It was well-patronized, well-lighted, and possessed of a genial patron who spoke good English: though that did not really matter given that James could speak Dutch. Most tables were occupied but the proprietor found one for us near the bar. James ordered a round of a special Dutch aperitif that he was anxious for us to try. While we all sampled this local spirit thawing us out from the day's frigidity, he and Patricia closely discussed the menu. Eventually, a meal was ordered… and more drinks.

Beaming at us, making us clink glasses, James surveyed us fondly. He began, 'It's so good to have you both here for the festive season. Usually nobody comes.' He was soon getting gushy, sentimental. 'Yes, my dears, I'm so happy…' Then, abruptly, James fell forward and toppled off his chair onto the floor. It was a spectacular passing out. Theatrical. Once more time stopped, as that terrible feeling of anxiety again gripped Patricia and me, as it had done the day he collapsed on the country lane back in Brixham. In a second our little relaxed *tête-à-tête* had blown up into a bubble inflated with tension gas. Then, from a neighbouring table, a woman with an American accent came and knelt beside James. She loosened his collar, felt for a pulse, and informed us she was a nurse. Moments later, which seemed much longer, the pulse being there, James opened his old blue eyes and looked into those of the nurse. 'Am I dead?' he demanded. 'Naht at all!' said the woman jokily. 'Seeing you, my dear, I thought you were an angel and that I must be dead!' retorted our friend the poet.

A cushion was produced by the proprietor and placed beneath James's head to make him more comfortable. The proprietor then 'phoned for paramedics who arrived with commendable speed. James was very apologetic to us and everyone. He tried to talk his way out of the situation. But the paramedics insisted on taking him, and us, to the hospital. The only consolation to James seemed to come when one of the paramedics informed him that Queen Beatrix of the Netherlands was in the same hospital that day for an operation. 'Something to tell my Dutch chums about!' he observed consolingly.

For most of the afternoon that Boxing Day, Patricia and I sat in the waiting room of the Casualty Department of the chief hospital in Den Haag. A very boring, as well as anxious, wait. Finally, we were permitted to visit James in a ward. He was lying stretched out on a bed fully clothed and somewhat subdued. Still annoyed with himself, but rather weary now. Amazingly, though, he handed us a sheaf of notes he'd written out while waiting to see us. He also gave us a key to his flat and some money. He insisted we returned to the flat in the Riouwstraat, feed ourselves and read the notes, 'So you'll know what to do if I die in the night.' Charming, I thought. What a bloody Christmas!

Burdened thus, we went back to the apartment knowing that we still had some days of our stay to complete before going back to England. Later that evening James was brought home from the hospital by taxi. He looked tired, and was clearly shaken by his misfortune. He wanted no food and was desperate to have a bath and retire to bed. Both of which he soon managed. It was hard, though, for his guests to sleep that night for worrying what they might find the next morning. Sir Jim alive, or Sir Jim dead?

But there he was the following morning, up as bright as a sparrow, and insisting that – as had been arranged – we three should set off for Amsterdam to meet his old friend Katrina. But, as he soon found he was not up to it, he packed Patricia and I off to Delft so he could have a day's rest. We'd all go to Amsterdam the day after instead, he said. So we two went off to Delft – a city famous for pottery and a huge windmill – and while we had a pleasant uneventful day there, it was difficult not to keep wondering how things were with our host back in The Hague.

But came the next day to go to Amsterdam, James was still not up to it. Though he was absolutely insistent on coming to the railway station to see us off. He offered first to drive us to the train; but we said no, we liked going on the trams. He knew, of course, we were fearful of the consequences of his driving in his condition. We denied his suggestion that we thought he might collapse at the steering wheel. But it was that, of course. In the end we all took the tram to the station, where he bought us return tickets to Amsterdam, gave us a letter for Katrina (which turned out to contain money), and, anxious as a mother hen over her brood, saw us off.

By prearrangement ostentatiously carrying a copy of Patricia's journal *Acumen*, in which some of James's translations appeared, we met the vigorous Katrina. She was an angular-faced Dutchwoman, with dark dyed hair, probably around seventy years of age. She escorted us straight to the Rijksmuseum that we might view, inter alia, Rembrandt's remarkable 'Nightwatch' painting, together with a whole crop of Van Gogh's. After which, we visited a market where Katrina bought eels and smoked salmon for lunch.

Katrina dwelt in a tall, very narrow house near the canal network of this 'Venice of the North'. It was a gloomy, somewhat threadbare place that she had occupied with her late husband for many years. Her husband was a German artist of some repute, and they had been there from before the Nazi occupation of the country. Since her husband's death, she had spent her time looking after his archive. It seems he was an artist of sufficient importance – he was a cartoonist – to have attracted the attention of Hermann Goering. The artist was a known left-winger and, according to Katrina, Goering pronounced to him, 'You will not be shot for your opposition to the New Germany. Instead, you will go to prison until we have won the war.'

On the top floor of the thin house was a studio room with skylight. There we lunched on salmon and eel and drank wine. As Katrina's English was excellent, a wide-ranging discourse between us wound its way through the afternoon. In the evening, despite heavy rain, we walked along the banks of seemingly endless canals. Finally, we arrived at a restaurant which had once been a police station. A building which, claimed Katrina, was where Napoleon's army had stabled horses. It had the air and simplicity of stables: bare wooden floors and heavy, light-coloured chairs. But the food and wine were excellent. There we stayed with this stranger who lavishly entertained us on James's money – 'James is so generous!' she continued to exclaim – until it was time to get the train back to Den Haag where we found James seemingly fully recovered and eager for us to give a full account of our visit. It seemed he had sent Katrina a thousand guilder note.

Early the following morning we said our farewells to Sir Jim. Still in his dressing gown, his blue eyes moist, his handshake less vigorous than when we had arrived, but his personality beginning to bubble once more like cooled water starting to boil. We climbed into the taxi, James giving the driver strict directions as to which of Den Haag's stations we were to be taken to. I have to say Patricia and I sank back into the taxi's seats with a sense of relief. Relief not only at the thought that distance must inevitably diminish our sense of anxiety about our friend's health – if only because it would not be constantly before our gaze. And, for sure, we felt the return journey just had to be more hassle-free than our outward one on Christmas Eve.

Everything did, indeed, go smoothly from Den Haag to Brussels. The only slight irritant came on reaching the Eurostar departure gate in Brussels. There we found a full airport-style radar checking security system in place, unlike on our outward journey. No automatic waving through of EC passport holders. I observed to Patricia, 'Clearly when the Belgians aren't on strike, their security system is much more rigorous than the British.' Eventually, though, we got through it all. The train left more or less on time. And though it was only mid-morning, I opened a bottle of *vin rouge* for the journey.

Then something happened at Liege, the last stop before the train enters the Channel Tunnel. A young woman boarded the train, placed a carrier bag on the rack above, and sat down next to a man in the seats directly in front of us. Shortly before the train left Liege she got up and disappeared down the carriage in the direction of the buffet bar. I forgot about her. Everyone forgot about her. Until, that is, the Eurostar was racing towards the tunnel.

One of the train hostesses suddenly appeared in our carriage and began going from seat to seat addressing passengers. It seemed she was checking that each piece of luggage had an owner. When she reached the man in the seat in front of us she asked him to identify his luggage. He pointed to a briefcase on the luggage rack. 'And the carrier bag?' the hostess said. It was not his he replied. Whose then? He didn't know. I interposed and mentioned the young woman. Had she gone to the buffet? More uneasily: had she got back off the train at Liege? No one knew. But the entire carriage had gone suddenly quiet. The hostess spoke into a walkie-talkie. Almost immediately she was joined by a man in braided uniform.

Carefully the guard took the carrier bag off the rack and peered gingerly into it. The plastic bag contained a sealed packet. Without a word it was taken away by the man. Simultaneously, the train plunged into the tunnel under the English Channel. No one was now talking in the train carriage. 5 minutes. 10 minutes. 15 minutes. Then the train hostess and a ticket collector came back. Without a word the bag was put back on the luggage rack. Obviously it was okay. But what had they been looking for?

Later, when the ticket collector came to check everyone's tickets, I asked him what it had all been about. He explained that a leading member of a Protestant paramilitary organization had been murdered in the Maze Prison in Northern Ireland the previous weekend. A Christmas present, as it were, from the Provisional IRA. Security throughout the U.K. was being tightened up after threats to rail, air and sea networks – especially to the prestigious Eurostar service between London and the Continent.

The train came out of the Channel Tunnel into the sunlight of Kent – the Garden of England. At which moment Patricia and I nodded off with sheer relief. Christmas away from home was over. And just before the train entered Waterloo Station we both came to. In the seat in front of us was the missing owner of the carrier bag reading a magazine. But for my chivalrous nature, I could have hit her over the head with my rolled newspaper!

3.
A POET'S FUNERAL

My friend Tony is a businessman who runs a successful firm in Oxford. He has a holiday home in The Mount. We have been friends for years. Not a literary man, Tony has, on account of our friendship (and his wife), found himself constrained to take an interest in poets – *forced by circumstance* he would no doubt argue! Every time he reads an obituary of a poet in the newspapers, he sends me a cutting accompanied by the words 'Another one gone – drink again!' Though not a poet himself, like I say, he has a lively interest in death.

Somewhere around his fiftieth birthday, Tony said to me – I think it was one of those halcyon summer evenings in The Golden Lion on Brixham's New Road –'I find the first thing I turn to in the newspapers these days is the obituaries,' he paused, 'It must be my age. I find a lot of my friends do the same.' Like I say, he has a lively interest in death. In fact, to try and mitigate the inevitable impact on himself of the Grim Reaper, Tony retired at fifty. Unfortunately, in his own words, he discovered after six months that he was 'irreplaceable' in both his own business and in his own eyes. Though I suspect that the truth was he grew so bored with tinkering with his vintage Bentley, and the heating systems in various houses, that this modest discovery of his own commercial indispensability was but an excuse. That, and the fact he dimly perceived like the sculptor Rodin that it is not sex or money but work which provides the best escape from death. At least, work puts out of mind the almost daily threats of mortality; and one never knows but that keeping really busy might just make one late for one's own funeral.

Now death it was, too, and a poet or, rather, the death of a poet, that leads to another more episodic memory involving Tony. Tony that is, and his really nice wife Fran. They have been married longer than chalk and cheese, and have a loving scepticism towards each other that Tony – to the merriment of his friends – translates into a real Irish stew of hyperbole and fib, with the occasional seasoning of classic self-pity. Fran is very forbearing, but Tony – as he will tell you – is 'the tolerant one'.

But to the little episode of the poet Sally Purcell's funeral. I did not know the deceased poet well, but had gone to the funeral at the suggestion of Peter Jay, her publisher, who assumed because I published a number of Sally's poems in an anthology I edited that she and I were friends. In fact, I only met her once, and then briefly at the Oxford launch of that anthology in St. Peter's College. The funeral service was at the Oratory in St. Giles.

Unfortunately, because Patricia was supervising the installation of a new kitchen back at our house in Brixham, my wife and literary partner was unable to accompany me to the funeral. Like me, she had not known Sally Purcell beyond her poetry and a reputation for being somewhat fey, much in the way that the Christina Rossetti of 'Goblin Market' seems fey to us. Not quite 'away with the fairies' but almost. Certainly Sally came over strongly in her poetry as a mental traveller in the medieval landscapes of Sir Gawain and the Green Knight. Also, at our one meeting she seemed a highly neurotic, dowdy yet ethereal being, only a few degrees short of owning a broomstick. Sensitive and mysterious.

Anyway, I took myself off the evening prior to the funeral to Boar's Hill, Oxford where I stayed overnight with Tony and Fran. I remember telling them of the nightmare Christmas Patricia and I had just spent in Holland as the guest of a delightful old poet full of energy, but given to spectacular collapses in public places. While Fran countered with the somewhat more mundane subject of a new house she had bought in North Oxford and which she was keen for me to see.

The next morning, after sharing hangovers at breakfast, Fran drove me to see this house which she was having renovated. Her husband is the supreme DIY man among my friends; and in his hands it doesn't mean 'Destroy It Yourself'. To describe the new house as an unexceptional Sixties' style house is to praise it. A modern, nondescript, redbrick terraced house that may have had a flat roof. 'Yes, er, very nice.' I said to Fran, swallowing as little of her enthusiasm as decency would permit. Then we drove off in search of the Oratory church. Up and down the Woodstock Road, in and out St. Giles. In the end we stopped the car and asked a street cleaner. 'Oh, yeah, that's St. Aloysius's wot yer wants. Over there, mate.' He knew, as I had suspected he might. The notice board outside the church said in large letters 'St. Aloysius' Church' and, in diminutive lettering in small brackets '(The Oratory)'.

Had this, in the dim and distant past, been a takeover of one church by another? We didn't know. But the two names had cost us an extra half hour's driving. As it turned out, however, it didn't matter because the Oratory was not yet open for burying, praying, hymning or anything else.

Fran dropped me at the kerbside in St. Giles's, drove off and I walked straight into an Army Recruiting Office in the belief that it was a café. No one pointed a rifle at me, but if they had I couldn't have left quicker than I did. I have no objections to death, I just didn't want to sign up to be a cause of it. Writing poems is quite stressful enough.

As I turned down the street away from the Recruiting Office, I ran into Fred Beake and Douglas Clark – two poets from the city of Bath. They were going for a coffee, so I joined them. Fred is a Yorkshire type with the appearance of an Old Testament prophet and has the only voice I have encountered that can grind words to powder on occasion. Douglas on the other hand is the taller of the two – a man from County Durham with a mild Scots' accent: he wears spectacles that he likes frequently to move up and down his forehead like he was fixing a second pair of eyes on himself. He is a likeable, clerkly figure who was a computer expert or paid nerd at Bath University for many years.

We turned into a 'greasy spoon' type of café, and there discovered Eddie Linden and John Heath-Stubbs already at a table, so we joined them. Eddie and John had been well-known fixtures on the London literary landscape for many years. John was a giant of a man, totally blind by then, who resembled a large, grey statue. When he laughed, he threw his head back and giggled loudly to the ceiling. Eddie, by contrast, was a small man like an old-fashioned warped cricket bat. A temperamental Scot, he was given to telling everyone within hearing that he was 'gay, socialist and Roman Catholic!' The latter a combination that not infrequently nonplussed his auditors who – fools that they were – expected some degree of consistency to validate human utterances. This highly colourful Scotsman had been his blind friend's eyes (not ears) for many years, steering Heath-Stubbs around the country to poetry readings and literary parties. John was a considerable poet of great learning and it was an honour to be one of his acolytes *.

---

* John Heath-Stubbs, OBE, died in 2006 aged 88 – *Editor.*

As we finished our coffees and prepared to walk the couple of hundred yards to the church, John expressed a wish to visit the toilet before we left. 'Will ye take him William? It's doonstairs. 'Am nae so big an' ye can handle him better.' So 'doonstairs' to the toilets I took him. When we returned to the café from the basement our companions, including the ever loyal Eddie, had left. So my steering of the Bard of Notting Hill had to continue all the way to the church. Where, when we arrived, slightly late, and I had to force the big door open by great effort which led to an even greater noise, the entire congregation swivelled heads at us. Only the priest remaining motionless, his back to us and arms raised towards the altar. Our entry signalled the start of the Requiem Mass for Sally Purcell poet, lecturer in Medieval French and part-time barmaid at the nearby King's Head public house.

It was at The King's Head afterwards that the wake for Sally was held; and Eddie, whose great caring skills had somehow failed to find transport for himself and John (everyone it seemed had left their cars at the out-of-town park-and-ride places), it again fell to me to get them to the pub. By taxi.

Peter Jay of Anvil Press, Sally's publisher, Eddie, John, me, Douglas Clark, Fred Beake, Kit Wright, the late William Cookson, editor of that fine magazine *Agenda*, who was about to 'come off the wagon' and begin his last great drinking spree before his liver gave out and he ceased to be a liver, plus Val Warner who was a leading authority on the Edwardian poetess Charlotte Mew who, like Sylvia Plath but forty years earlier, committed suicide. Many others too whom I cannot now recall toasted Sally the Departed in her favourite pub.

For some very odd reason to me, who that day utterly failed to organize myself, fell the task of getting various of the inebriated mourners' journeys home arranged. I went and brought a taxi from St. Giles's to take John Heath-Stubbs and Fred Beake to the London train – Beake was not going home to Bath that day. Then I had to get Eddie Linden to Oxford Station: for some reason Eddie didn't want to go back to London with John. Finally, at about 6.30pm, (the wake had begun about 1pm.), it occurred to me to ask myself where I was supposed to be going? Or, rather, Peter Jay wondered where I was to spend the night: enquired whether I was staying over in Oxford or going back to Devon that evening? Even then it was not for a while before I remembered that I was supposed to ring Fran, 'At work before 5.30pm. Or at home not later than 6.30pm.' It was another while before I could ring either place on the pub payphone – and then only with the kindly assistance of an Oxford legal don who had the requisite skills to understand the thing. Needless to say, it wasn't long before I discovered I had lost contact with my Boar's Hill hosts.

As I partook of another drink, as the Irish would say, I recalled that it had been their intention to take me to The Butcher's Arms in Headington, followed by 'a curry' somewhere. Brilliant! I was saved. I knew what to do. After taking an unsteady farewell of Peter and the legal don, I resorted yet again to the taxi rank in St. Giles. 'Where to, mate?' 'The Busher's Arms, pleesh.' 'Which Butcher's Arms? There's more than one.' 'Er, oh, the one at Headington.'

The Butcher's Arms is embedded in a large housing estate. And all estates are brick mazes designed to defeat everyone, especially poets and rent collectors. Pubs are their only landmarks and taxi drivers at least know them. So, eventually, I walked into The Butcher's Arms, having paid my fare and, as the cliché has it, found 'the place was heaving'. It was like Saturday night in a Wild West saloon and I was a stranger just in town. Only a stranger in this case to whom nobody paid any attention. What could I do but shove my way to the bar; which I finally reached after a procession of 'excuse mes' and 'thank yous' mixed with the occasional 'watch it mate!' from the odd disgruntled drunk. As I was about to order at the bar, a voice screeched like a parrot behind me, 'It's the poet!'. Momentarily a shocked silence fell on those drinkers around me. Filled with wine and initiative I, too, looked around to see if I could spot a poet. I couldn't. Only my own red visage in the mirror behind the bar.

Out of the press of bodies and faces emerged Jackie. Then Dennis. Who were they? How did I know them? Friends of Tony and Fran. What do they look like? Jackie is an articulate, afro-looking woman with silvery hair like a close-fitting Roman helmet. Dennis, a stocky guy with a beard, is a jazz fan who frequently makes about as much sense to his fellow humans as does his favourite music to a classical music buff. Which is to say that his outlook on life is decidedly improvisatory. He appears shocking or mad by turns even to his wife. But one can't help liking them, as I do, and it was they who rescued me that evening. As Tony was to later put it, 'Jackie and Dennis are good at taking in stray dogs. And there's not much difference with poets.'

However, before the three of us rattled off unsteadily to Jackie and Dennis's luxury bungalow to meet their ferociously-loveable dog Chloe, plus a chicken roast, an attempt was made to locate Tony and Fran. This came about – the attempt that is – through another customer at the bar, who not only confirmed that my friends had been in the pub earlier looking for me, but also claimed that he 'knew' where they went for their Friday evening curries. This customer – who affirmed that he was 'Tony's technical director' – spent some time on his mobile phone ringing round various Indian restaurants that dot Oxford like curry temples. But to no avail. While Alan, as Tony's employee was called, carried out his telephone research I, to my amazement and no little surprise, was given a handful of tokens by Dennis to procure myself 'drinks on the house'. Not wishing to seem ungrateful, I did as invited.

To prove I was a poet and to sing for my supper, once we were at Jackie and Dennis's bungalow I was prevailed on to give a poetry reading. This I did. And there survives a photograph taken by Jackie showing the mightily muscular small dog Chloe with one of my feet in its mouth, while I read aloud from a book in my hand. Indeed, it's an odd thing that – the poet and dog 'thing'. At a reading I once gave in Kentish Town I had canine assistance of a sort there too. Throughout my reading – delivered from a small dais – a dog with one of its legs in plaster of Paris insisted on walking up and down throughout: *clumpertyclumpertyclumpertyclump* (as James Joyce would have rendered it) – a sound much at variance with my pentameters.

Fairly late on I rang the house on Boar's Hill to let Tony and Fran – whom I rightly assumed would be home by then – know my whereabouts. Said Tony, who answered the phone, 'I told Fran you'd turn up sooner or later… You'd better stay where you are. We'll bring you a change of clothes in the morning, then take you to the station. After that, if you get lost on the way home it'll be Patricia's responsibility. Goodnight!'

It's nice to have friends I always say.

4.
THE '59 CLUB

It is strange how many things one gets involved with in a lifetime: things that you never forget, yet which lead nowhere. In the late 1950s a group of public school boys – young chaps really – formed this club. There were girls of like ilk who were members of it too. The club met periodically in a private room in premises in Beak Street, W.1. Patricia and I – unwed then – were the sole persons of ordinary background, and a non-public school education, who were members of it at first. This all came about through my friend Tom whom I had met at work. We were both articled clerks in the offices of a Manchester accountancy firm.

Tom was a remarkable young man. He was the son of an imperial businessman who had, amongst many interests, once owned *The Rangoon Times* of Burma. Tom's mother and father had a rather grand house in Cheshire. It was a residence always open to friends – including Tom's youthful chums – and his parents were the last people I knew who kept servants: gardeners, cooks and a chauffeur called, believe it or not, Monsieur Leotard. Though indulgent of her son and his friends, Tom's mother considered me somewhat precocious and possessed of 'too many opinions for his age'. But the trouble was that Tom had every bit as many opinions as me; so his mother couldn't complain too much. As for Tom's other traits: he had an endlessly ebullient nature and a genius for friendship. He influenced me in those ways, and doubtless in others too. It was only his liberal-radical outlook that I didn't share. His constant attempts to wean me away from my instinctive conservatism, or whatever it was, singularly failed. I embraced, however, his generosity of outlook towards his fellow men. Like Tom, I have never disliked a person on sight, not even a dentist. One can, of course, go off people; but in my case not before making their acquaintance.

Tom used to gather up groups of friends from the Manchester area and transport them to other parts of the country, simply in order to meet other sets of his friends – often ones who had been at Uppingham School with him. Usually the other parts of Britain to which we went – in Minis, Morris Minors, Spitfires, and Triumphs: all popular cars of the time – were in the south. London's Belgravia or Chelsea were popular destinations for Tom's Mancunian cavalcade of bright young things. Later, among other 'commoners' who accompanied Tom, was a flashy young man called Keith who was madly progressive in all things; and a thin, pasty-faced Jewish lad called David. Among the *hoi aristoi* I recall an Asquith descendent called Bob and a terribly posh young man with fair hair and haunted features called Nick Noel-Tod. Years later I saw the latter being led by a poodle or pekinese down Bond Street. The one I best remember, however, went by the somewhat theatrical name of Edwin Crump.

Well, some member of the '59 Club suggested we all went down to Brighton and Hove. What was proposed was that Tom would bring his friends from Manchester on a Friday to London. In the capital we would all be entertained in Beak Street to supper. Since the opening of the M1 motorway it was a much quicker journey south than before. We would, after the supper, doss down at various club members' London houses. Then the next day head off for Brighton.

Just to give a flavour of these jaunts – it may not have been on that particular occasion – I recall four of us and a load of luggage being jammed into a vintage, four-seater: a vehicle almost as old as the century. Such, however, was the amount of luggage that Patricia and I had to stand up in the back of the open-topped motor car. As we were going round Hyde Park Corner in this sedate but antique vehicle we were pulled up by the police. We explained that we were visitors to the capital. So the policeman made us sit with big suitcases on our knees; then, after giving us a caution, waved us on our unsteady way.

First, though, on the Saturday morning, we had to get a key to the house where we were to stay in Hove. This was known to entail a visit to the Savoy Hotel in the Strand where, it seemed, the father of one of Tom's friends kept a suite or something. Such a visit meant, as Tom said, 'A chap's got to wear a tie to get into the Savoy'. Needless to say, of course, not only had Tom forgotten a tie, but none of we casually-dressed hearties could muster a single one among us. So we received short-shrift at the main Strand entrance to the hotel, and were sent round to the tradesmen's entrance at the rear overlooking the Thames. Eventually, we were brought a key by some lackey.

In the middle of that same day, as part of Tom's entourage, we finally drove up the drive of a house of considerable proportions in

Hove. A beautiful house with a wide terrace of Cotswold stone and many acres of well kept garden. The dwelling was fully and beautifully furnished; and had I owned it I would have trembled to let it to a rabble of youth, no matter how well-brought-up. At any rate, we had free run of the place for the entire weekend, together with ample stocks of food and drink. Though whether we brought our own supplies or raided Sir and Lady Bountiful's stores, again I don't recall. But I do recall that we ate as much as stomachs needed, and drank far more than stomachs required!

It proved a fun weekend, as young people today would say. Then, language could be more localized. Members of the '59 Club had their own jargon – at least the more upper crust chaps and chapesses did. 'Oh, spit!' signified frustration; and 'Oh, sick!' more frustration still. As for, 'How sick-making!' that meant something was regarded as disgusting, even though it might be nothing more than that the ice for the gin-and-tonics had run out. There were other arcane and often silly-sounding sayings, now forgotten, but on the lips of some pretty debutante they were more charming than pretentious; while coming from a male law student or trainee accountant they sounded very affected... as, of course, they were intended to do.

A perfect summer evening, August. A hot night wrapping lawns, flowerbeds, walkways, hedges and the big house that was not ours. An unheated house with French windows open onto a terrace. Non-stereophonic, gramophone music playing like in some Noel Coward play. Young folk lounging on sofas, in armchairs, talking, 'putting the world to rights'. Others outside, wandering in pairs over the sloping-away-to-sea lawn, or being quietly intimate in shadows. The generation on the verge of the Sixties' Revolution, still trusted by parents – *just*! It was all a bit like Fournier's *Lost Domain*, only we were older than his characters.

The house was big but there were a lot of us. I think, too, a commitment had been given not to occupy the main bedroom. This resulted in some of us sleeping on floors in sleeping bags, or on sofas, or yawning all night in armchairs. I may have done the latter; flashman Keith certainly did. While Tom, immaculate in blazer and corduroys slept all night on a spread out copy of *The Times* on the ballroom floor. Youthfully eccentric, Tom was a laugh a minute. Dear Tom, who passed out of this world far too soon.

Before retiring for the night to our various quarters and postures, the egregious Edwin Crump seeing me crossing the lawn alone came up to me, 'Look, Will, old chap, I really like Patricia. I know she's your fiancé, but can I have her for one night? After all, you'll have her soon for the rest of your jolly vie, what?'

Completely taken aback, I blurted, 'No, you can't!'

Edwin looked at me frowningly. He was about an inch or so taller than me, gangly in his limbs, with a distinctly square cranium and a semi-serious expression. After considering my rejection of his request for a few moments, he said, 'Alright, old man, how about I fight a duel with you for her?'

'A duel?' I was dumbfounded as they say.

'That's right,' he affirmed, 'and you can choose the weapons.'

I couldn't really believe what I was hearing. But always a bit sharp-tempered I bristled, 'Alright... fists then!'

'Fists it is and at dawn... well, let's say eight o'clock. Before brekkers, eh?'

I agreed and left him. I was stunned. What sort of people were these? Had a few hours in this old house somehow shoved the clock back a couple of centuries or what? I went and sought out Patricia and told her of Edwin's proposal.

'A duel over me?' She sounded not so much alarmed as impressed.

After a ridiculously wakeful night, at 8am most had at last fallen asleep, save Edwin and me. 'Keith's asleep.' I grumbled. My opponent agreed that his second was also as knocked out as Keith. Though they had both excitedly sworn the previous evening they'd be at our sides at dawn. So who was going to referee or witness this ridiculous charade?

My opponent looked nervously about him, as if he expected the Law to arrive any minute. Maybe he did? After all, Edwin had been one of the other passengers in the overloaded vintage Bentley which, the previous day, the police had pulled up at Hyde Park Corner (or was it Sloane Square? After so many years I grow unsure.) Eventually, Edwin spoke again. What he said was just as eccentric and incongruous as the business of fighting a duel in the middle of the Twentieth Century.

'Look, Will,' he began confidentially, 'I've been thinking during the night. You know I have got this glass eye?' It was something everyone knew. 'Well, your father was a boxer, Tom said. So, if we have a set-to, I might jolly well lose the other eye. And I couldn't really qualify as an accountant if I'm blind. So would you awfully mind if we called the duel off?'

In the distance I could see Patricia staring at us through the half-open French windows. I agreed, 'On one condition, okay? That you turn your back on me and walk away from the direction of the house.'

This my putative opponent readily did. Whilst I strolled casually back up the sloping lawn to the stone terrace with its ornamental balustrade.

'Not much of a duel.' observed my spouse-to-be ironically.

'He chickened out.'

'Why?'

'Didn't want to risk losing his good eye.'

For a few moments Patricia looked at me with a trace of suspicion on her face. She had a habit then of wrinkling her slightly snubbed nose when doubtful of something. Then, I guess, having seen Edwin push off so hastily, she accepted it was probably the truth I was telling her.

Such are the sort of things that happened to members of the '59 Club all those lost years ago. Happenings – to use a soon-to-be-fashionable expression of the 1960's — which led nowhere. Happenings, like the friendships made there, ephemeral. Save, of course, my friendship with Tom which, like his with me, could never have been ephemeral: it was too intense for that. Even so, that friendship also led nowhere but to the grave.

But the other friendships, well, the story is similar. For example, in recent years Keith turned up in Torbay as the owner of one of our major hotels. In fact, as it turns out – courtesy of an internet search engine – the owner of a string of hotels. I spotted his picture in the local paper and still recognized him despite the passage of time. I rang him up to check he was the original Keith of Tom's group of ubiquitous '59ers. Yes, he was, and how clever of me to recognize him, says he. Did he want a drink with a bit of his past? I ask. Sorry, too busy.

Like I say, so many things there are one gets involved in which lead nowhere.

5.
LOST IN LLANDRINDOD

Llandrindod Wells – to give the place its full name – is approximately half-way along the railway line that runs from Swansea to Shrewsbury. It toddles along through the most luminous green country that is the heart of Wales; and is single track for most of the way. Mid-Wales, with its tree-tufted hills and sweat of silvery streams, is very beautiful and is, like Greece, a landscape mapped by myth. Myths redolent of King Arthur; myths famously collected together in the stories of *The Mabinogion*. But like so many places to which I have been, I've gone there at the behest of others. Friends who say, 'You must come and see…etc.' Usually they have been right. The initiative for the trip to Llandrindod came from my old friend Glyn Pursglove who then lived with his Persian wife and young daughters in Swansea, where he taught at the university. He is retired now and his daughters have partners; and his wife, Parvin, continues to work on Anglo-Persian translating.

It was during one of our visits to stay with them at their house in Brynmill – where Dylan Thomas grew up – that it was suggested we all went off for the day to visit Llandrindod because Glyn felt it was a place we should 'definitely experience'. He made it sound mystical. Staying with Glyn and Parvin at the time were two Austrians, Wolfgang and his girlfriend Andrea. Wolfgang was an academic from the University of Salzburg who, some years later, was to become the editor of *Poetry Salzburg Review*, a distinguished international English-language journal devoted to poetry. It was decided we would make up a party and have a long and, hopefully, jolly day out. Leaving very early in the morning on the little, two-carriage train, we rattled along merrily beneath a grey, rain-filled sky towards Shrewsbury. Though, of course, we were not going all that way: only about three hours' worth of journey along that mostly single track, iron way: a journey that ended for us at the spa town of Llandrindod Wells.

Temporarily, for passing purposes, the railway line bifurcates into two parallel tracks at Llandrindod. This is to enable the Swansea train to meet up with and pass the train from Shrewsbury: a fact that was to become significant much later in the day. But I only mention the double track here because it necessitates a bridge for passengers to cross from one platform to the other. A bridge which we were all crossing in brilliant sunlight (a temporary condition of the Welsh weather as it was to turn out) when an extraordinary thing happened.

In the nearby station car park, which the bridge overlooked, a parked car suddenly exploded into flames like in some disaster movie. Car alarms are often triggered by a sudden spell of hot weather, such as occurred at that moment with the parting of the clouds. But never had any of us seen a car explode through heat. We all lingered on the iron bridge for a while, watching the vehicle blazing away merrily. Was it perhaps the work of terrorists – Welsh Nationalists? I wondered. No one knew. Glyn shook his head and said with feeling, 'See what damage sun can do!' adding, 'I always say rain is better for us.' Andrea, an Italianate sun-worshipper from the south of Austria, stared at Glyn in disbelief. Only an Englishman (and Glyn was from Yorkshire) could entertain such a silly notion! As I say, it is Glyn's love of out-of-the-way places, like his love for minor and neglected poets of the past, that had brought us to Llandrindod, Walter Savage Landor country. It was soon enough, too, that he was to get his wish for rain as a real Welsh deluge was about to begin.

Fortunately, just as the first large, godlike tears fell, we were in among the trees of a small wood set in the town park, making our way hurriedly along a path towards the spa house: a sort of glass rotunda which incorporated a restaurant. The building was, in fact, mostly constructed of glass and ironwork, with a covered veranda running round the outside. As one entered the main door, one was immediately confronted by a huge, polished long bar like in a Wild West saloon. On this bar's vastness stood a single pump-handle with a handwritten card propped up next to it which read:10p per glass. This was the spa water on sale.

Having walked the full length of the bar we entered the restaurant. It felt like a sort of Food Morgue. The whole place resembled a disused 18th century ballroom, and it was deathly quiet. On the sea-huge floor, various tables were dotted about, mostly occupied by elderly figures, who looked like cut out shapes from an album of Edwardian photographs. Antique colonels with rubicund faces and deaf aids, together with their expressionless wives, leaned over great white bowls of soup or wrestled with roast dinners. The only words I heard spoken was by one of the ladies who muttered something through clenched teeth which sounded like, 'Must you darling?' Presumably her husband had said or done something indecorous. You could tell how far gone these restaurant regulars were when they showed no interest in our party, even though we had two of those minatory beings with us often described with fear and loathing as 'other people's kids'. It was like dining in Madame Tussaud's waxworks.

Even so, we were served and we did eat a reasonable lunch. While another waxen figure, dressed in a blazer like many of the others, appeared from a door in the wall and began to play old-fashioned tunes on an upright piano. The most obvious word to apply to this Welsh pagoda half-hidden by wet Welsh trees is that much misused Anglo-Saxon term 'weird'. And those of us brave enough to lash out ten pence for the spa water felt doubly weird after trying it. One of the children, the elder, and myself shared a glassful – taking one mouthful each, grimacing horribly, then putting it down. Everyone else fell back on personal prejudices, condemning it untasted with, 'Ugh! No thanks.'

During the meal, and for some time afterwards, the rain thundered down on the dome-shaped roof. It was real Welsh rain which, seemingly, beating even Manchester downpours: to adopt the wine bibber's labelling, it was Vintage Rain. So, for a while, it seemed we were trapped in the place. But, eventually, boredom got the better of the bad weather and most began to take Glyn's more positive view of the deluge – even our two Austrians – summed up in asseverations like 'What the hell? It's only water anyway.' And they all prepared to leave, save myself who was happy to stay on awhile reading a pamphlet on the poetry of Dylan Thomas which Glyn had presented me with. This I did; and the rest left, Glyn advising me to, 'Follow when you wish. Llandrindod's a small enough place. You can't get lost. We'll have a look around then see you in the bar of The White Hart.' Which sounded a fine arrangement to me; and I settled in a wicker, cushioned chair on the veranda to read the pamphlet, sparing the occasional glance at the dripping wet branches in this ornamental Arthurian glade – as I fancied it to be.

In one of Plato's Socratic dialogues is considered the question as to whether pleasure or thought produces the most happiness. I do not feel myself a great thinker; nor am I a much practiced hedonist; but I do enjoy a good ruminate: a reverie or a read or both in my own time and my own space, or someone else's. I did enjoy that post-prandial hour in that odd venue.

Next, though, there followed a systematic but somewhat disquieting search of the town for my wife and friends. Despite Glyn's claim that the town of Llandrindod Wells was too small for anyone to get lost in, my searching kept drawing blanks. Even the aforementioned White Hart was shutting by the time I located it, and they were not there. Then I spotted a bookshop. Eureka – that's where they would be! But, in fact, going into that tidy bookshop merely further separated me from my companions, as I temporarily began browsing among the tomes and forgot them. I even browsed so far as to purchase a book. Not, of course, an unusual thing for me to do in a bookshop; but a foolish thing just then, as was soon to become apparent to myself.

It was gone 4 o'clock in the afternoon when I left the book den, and I suddenly remembered – or thought I did (panic, panic) – that the train we were to take back to Swansea was supposed to depart at about ten past four, or 16.10pm. in timetable terms. I ran towards the station next to where the motor vehicle had blown up to welcome us to Llandrindod. When I reached the station I discovered what I already feared, the train had left five minutes earlier. The waiting-room-cum-foyer, like the platforms, was deserted. No sign at all of my wife and our friends. Bugger!

Not only had they gone and left me, but they had taken my ticket with them. Bugger number two! Yet surely not? I went to the ticket office and information window. Had the Swansea train really gone? It had – and 'on time' the very local official assured me with some pride. Bugger number three! But…but, er, had my friends by any chance left my ticket with him? He looked at me steadily, a man in official railway attire of black jacket, waistcoat and white shirt, then said in a slow Welsh accent, 'Now that's a first one, boyo, have they left your ticket with me? I've not heard that before!' I turned away from the window; walked a few paces; then went back again. 'How much is a single to Swansea?' 'Six pounds fifty pence leegal tender.' He said it with a hint of sarcasm, having quite made up his mind I was some sort of English rogue.

To say that I walked away disconsolately from the station at Llandrindod Wells is quite true. For, without even looking in my wallet, I knew that the purchase of the book had reduced my stock of cash below the ticket level. Bugger number four! (As to the title of the book, obviously being in denial about it still, I cannot recall it from that moment to this.) In those days, too, I had no 'plastic' and so could procure no money from a bank's cash machine.

Now, I must confess to having noticed a trait in my character: a trait that only ever appears in situations of crisis or threat. A characteristic which I can only describe as 'suicidal' – though more confidently knowledgeable folk might prefer a simpler term like 'stupidity'. At any rate, convinced now that I was lost in Llandrindod, on my own and abandoned by my friends, and lacking sufficient funds to get back to Swansea, I went into a coffee shop to spend some of those already dwindled funds. Indeed, I would have more welcomed an alcoholic beverage; but this being Wales in the 1980's, all decent hostelries were shut from 3pm to 7pm. My reasoning was that, well, if I hadn't enough cash for a train fare, I might as well spend some of it while I considered what to do. I even bought a cream cake as well as coffee to do a bit of 'comfort eating' while I puffed on my pipe and wondered whether there was likely to be such a person as an English consul in those parts who might get me repatriated – after all, Wales was a foreign country according to many wasn't it? The fact that I had been unable to find my friends in this small Welsh town – which I had thoroughly scoured for them – plus the fact that I was certain we'd all been intended to catch the ten past four train, had completely convinced me I really was on my own. Indeed, I might as well add that 'getting lost' was something of a habit with me: though for reasons that have never been apparent to me, I must say. Another instance of self-denial?

At about five thirty (Time again, boyo, see!) I had to leave the coffee shop as it was closing for the day. Not being able to think what else to do, with but three quid in my pocket by then, I wandered along the main street in the vague direction again of the station. In the street leading to the station was a public convenience. I thought it would give me something to do if I went there. As I drew near it – O wonder! O vision of a saviour! – I saw Glyn's wife Parvin coming out of the Ladies' toilet. Then, in solemn procession, first the women emerged from one exit; and Glyn and Wolfgang from the other. I was so relieved to see them: a different kind of relief from what I had expected at that place.

On every occasion when I have got lost, and am then re-discovered, I have noticed my friends always appear not quite as warm over the re-union as myself. Sometimes their feelings get enshrined in a pithy, even direct question like, 'Where the bloody hell have you been?' (That was when I got lost in Dublin in 1995.) Or like with my pal Tony a more resigned, 'We knew you'd turn up.' Yet others, like Patricia for example, are inclined to take what might be called a 'judicial' view of the matter, immediately putting me on trial in order to establish the exact extent of my always-presumed culpability, on the illegal principle of guilty before proved innocent. But I mustn't grumble. I was happy to 'take the stick' just for the joy of not having to hitch hike back to Swansea on £3. Much nicer, easier by train. Or would it be?

The station's waiting area, where the ticket office was also, was in the entrance foyer. Seats ran around the plain walls and they were mostly unoccupied, except for a totally silent, morose-looking man like a farmhand; and a middle-aged, matronly Welsh woman knitting some unrecognizable garment-to-be.

It was as we were all seated waiting in this echoing foyer that I learned of my timetable error. 'I thought we were supposed to be going back to Swansea on the 16.10?' I ventured. Glyn with his teacher's face on him that was one of patience with students and other idiots, 'No, I told you the 6.10 train – which is 18.10 European time.' After that I said nothing more about timetables.

Our Austrian friend, Wolfgang, in his wisdom had some packs of lager and packets of sausages and cheese. He said, 'We have these on the train, yes?' Everyone agreed. Meanwhile, the station clock read 6pm exactly.

'There's no train!' said a voice suddenly, sounding mildly triumphant, like that of someone who has answered a quiz question successfully.

In surprise we all looked at Blodwen the Knitter, or whatever the middle-aged lady might have been called. Before, however, the natural scholar in Glyn could ask her to 'name her sources' for this claim, she continued, ''Tis broken down, see, the train from Shrewsbury.' She seemed so certain nobody dared question her now; and the farming type shifting his pipe from one side of his mouth to the other; looked at her with rain-grey Welsh eyes. He accepted her wisdom too. So it had to be true because people love, most of all, contradicting others; and no attempt was made to challenge this Blodwen.

After a period of silence all round I felt we, at least, should alter focus. 'Let's have some of your picnic now, Wolfgang, what do you think?' This went down well, and we broke open the first of the six-packs of lager. It is surprising what a bit of food and drink can do: how it cheers and inspires, humour in people. We were soon feeling convivial, teasing the children, and even trying to shock the locals by offering the kids little sips of beer. But neither Blodwen the Knitter nor Jones the Farmer showed any signs of disapproval. Or of anything much. When, however, I asseverated, 'When the Swansea train arrives, the simplest thing to do would be to disembark all the passengers for Shrewsbury, and then let it take us all back to Swansea', the lady with the knitting put her wool and needles down on the seat beside her, and disappeared out onto the platform. My observation which, I see now, qualified for the selfish remark of the week, had had some effect. A minute or two later the woman returned, picked up her knitting, and said briefly to us, 'I've told Ewan.'

It seemed Ewan was the stationmaster; and while it was not entirely clear what she had told him, one deduced she had put my idea to the stationmaster. A fact that was soon empirically verified when several dozen passengers, evidently Shrewsbury-bound, were ordered off the train when it arrived from Swansea; and we were invited to board it by an unseen announcer over the loud-speaker system: presumably Ewan.

After that, there is not much more to tell. Assisted by Wolfgang's supply of food and drink, we pleasantly roistered the long journey back to Swansea through the ever deepening shades among the toy mountains — to Austrians Wolfgang and Andrea — of Wales. The tumultuous rain started up again bouncing down upon the dim fields and swelling streams and the occasional river that the train crossed on low metal bridges. Everyone was mellow and happy, feeling that the day had proved most enjoyable. In fact, nothing could go wrong to detract from our visit to Llandrindod Wells. And nothing did.

Yet a month afterwards we all had pause for thought when abruptly that innocuous rail line was thrust briefly into the national press. The two carriage train, crossing one of the little bridges over a much swollen river, had been pitched into those waters which had undermined the structure. Several passengers lost their lives.

It could so easily have been us.

6.
A YORKSHIRE LASS

During the period that we dwelt in student accommodation on the Finchley Road, Audrey Nicholson befriended us. Who was she? Good question. What she was, was a bespectacled woman in her sixties who, though thin-faced, severe and appropriately faded, was friendly, animated and sunny towards us. Why? Because she sensed we shared her love of poetry – which we did. Neither Patricia nor I can exactly remember how she swam into our ken. But my most distinct memory of her is that on one or more occasions she came to our rooms for lunch.

It was on these visits we gradually learned something of her. She was very proud of her northern origins – Yorkshire – and she was quite unfazed to discover we were Lancastrians. The Wars of the Roses had quite passed her by: she expected us to be, assumed we were, as naturally northern-oriented as she was. I recall she presented us with two books on her visits that perfectly expressed different sides of this literate lady. One was a joke book by a famous Lancashire comedian; the other was an obscure pamphlet of poetry by a poet whom neither Patricia nor I had heard of. This latter was kindly inscribed to us by the said poet whom neither of us knew. And it was only later we were to discover that it was Audrey's practice to buy quantities of the publications of any poets she approved of, and give away copies of them to friends and acquaintances of hers. Not a poet herself, it was her way of patronising and, as it were, repaying an art that had given her so much pleasure.

We discovered at the first luncheon at Finchley Road that she lived in a bedsit in Leytonstone and that she had taught at Berkeley University in California. That she had also been a teacher at various schools in Essex was not mentioned at that time, but it did explain her residence in Leytonstone when I later found this out. An additional fact that came out just then was that she had spent some time in Majorca acting as unpaid occasional secretary to Robert Graves back in the fifties.

As I write this it comes back to me that Audrey was also amanuensis to John Heath-Stubbs, and I recall how she and I first met. The circumstances were not propitious. At this time, and for many years before, I had been a visitor to John Heath-Stubbs' flat in Notting Hill. Visits that became more frequent during the period 1988-1992 when Patricia was at London University, and I was acting as her 'student's assistant'. Eddie Linden and Adam Johnson were John's main helpers – as I have said elsewhere John was blind – but I understood that a woman called Audrey would come in frequently to do typing for him. So it was inevitable I would run into her eventually. As I did, but under less than propitious circumstances.

One morning I went round to have coffee with John and, for once, discovered it was ready and waiting for me. The usual hassle of this proud, blind poet making coffee for me – he refusing all assistance – was, for once, obviated. There then ensued one of our pleasanter *débats* – I put it this way because all our conversations boiled down to my strongly interrupting a blind man's monologues, the result of which was we always kind of argued in the Greek sense of that word. But, at any rate, we were eventually interrupted by the arrival of his 'secretary'. To whom I was introduced.

However, Audrey was at that moment too agitated to really take much notice of myself. It seems that some criminals had been watching her flat and had, somehow, contrived to intercept her post and purloined a new cheque book sent by her bank. They had then started issuing cheques to buy things, signing the cheques in her name but without caring what her signature was like, knowing full well they could get away with it for some days before the first of the cheques were presented to her bank and the matter came to light.

Like I say, Audrey was much upset by all of this and spoke of it at great length: the torrent of her words forcing silence on John and myself for a while. Now, whether John had grown impatient or what, I don't know. What I do know was that he made some facetious utterance, accompanied by one of his little giggles. Unfortunately, this caught Audrey 'on the raw' as they say. And a very unpleasant and acrimonious scene ensued. The burden of which was Audrey reprimanding John, accusing him of callousness 'after all I've done for you!', etc. Somewhat overcome with embarrassment I quit the flat as soon as I could.

Sometime after that unfortunate encounter, Patricia and I became friends of Audrey's – that is, we were added to her huge circle of poets and poetry lovers – and I seem to recall Audrey took a shine to us at least in part because I had been witness to the row with Heath-Stubbs: almost as if she felt she had to make amends to me in some way by expunging the memory of that unfortunate incident in Notting Hill? Well, whatever, she gave Patricia and myself many pleasant literary hours together..

But, still, why do I feel obliged to write of her? Because I was fascinated to meet this aging woman of no privileged background who, it appeared, knew all the contemporary poets. Among the well-known living poets, Heath-Stubbs apart, she knew Gavin Ewart, Peter Porter, Dannie Abse, fellow Yorshireites Ken Smith and Ted Hughes, and Les Murray from way out in the Australian outback. There were many more than these whom Audrey Nicholson helped and promoted in all manner of ways. When she died *The Times* wrote of her, 'Blunt, unmarried and maternal not even in manner, Audrey Nicholson became like a mother to contemporary poetry…In person and in letters she rallied support for poetry readings and book launches and kept people informed of the triumphs of a famous poet or the need to send £5 to celebrate a poor one's birthday (the two were sometimes one)'.

It was no surprise then that when Patricia and I attended her funeral, some years after our extended sojourn in London had ended, so many other poets and poetasters turned up at the crematorium in Manor Park that some could not get into the chapel, and over half those who did, had to stand throughout the ceremony. And afterwards, at some pub on the edge of Wanstead Flats, it seemed half the poetry world was there for Audrey's wake. And I think this little anecdote following is appropriate to tell, and somehow illustrative of the important role women, who simply love poetry rather than write it, can play in the lives of poets.

I found myself at a table in the pub with John Rety and Susan Johns who run the Torriano reading centre for poetry. There was a woman with them whom I did not know. I had just been asked by Ken Smith if his long poem *Fox Running* had been listed in the *Long Poem Group Newsletter* which I was then co-editing with Sebastian Barker. I produced a copy, showed it him, and the woman with John and Susan asked to see it also. Included in the listings of long poems and sequences was Seamus Heaney's *Station Island*. Seeing this, the woman muttered her approval, adding she was pleased to see Ted Hughes' *Gaudette* was also listed. Then, extraordinarily, she said, 'Seamus always sends me all his poems for my opinion before he publishes them.' Now, why, I wondered should the famous Irish poet and Nobel prize-winner, Seamus Heaney, seek her approval of his poems? Who was she, this woman at Audrey Nicholson's funeral out on the Essex marshes? Eventually we were introduced. It was Olwyn Hughes, the sister of Ted Hughes, the latter being Seamus's best English friend. Suddenly, her claim did not seem far-fetched at all.

So this little anecdote made a kind of fitting conclusion to that day. For Patricia and I had met yet another woman – also from Yorkshire – who like Audrey was deeply embedded in the world of the Muse and her followers.

7.
SLEEPING WITH JOHN HEATH-STUBBS

A few years ago when Patricia ran a poetry day as part of the Ways With Words Festival at Dartington Hall I had to sleep with John Heath-Stubbs, that eminent blind bard, now, sadly, gone to Parnassus. This came about because the main organizers of the festival – who provided accommodation for performers – when they discovered Heath-Stubbs was blind, felt unable to arrange for him to be properly looked after. So they rang us at The Mount and, as Patricia was out shopping, I took the call, agreeing to take over responsibility for looking after John. The upshot of this was that, after several poets and ourselves in 6 The Mount there was no spare bed for John. So it was arranged that he and I would spend the night at No 4: Tony and Fran being absent. It was when the time came for us to retire for the night that things became interesting. Interesting…and difficult.

At No.4 there were twin beds: John having the one with his feet facing the door so that, if he wished to get to the toilet in the night, all he had to do was push his large frame to the end of the bed and walk out the door. There was a snag however. Immediately opposite the bedroom door were the stairs. To get to the bathroom and toilet one turned sharp right. An easy enough thing to do when one is sighted; although even a sighted person who was half-asleep and in unfamiliar surroundings could easily pitch down the stairs. Consequently, I arranged my bed so I could intercept our giant bard and steer him in the right direction. Fortunately, I am a light sleeper; though not quite the insomniac that the Bard of Notting Hill was.

The first little hiccup actually occurred before we had 'settled for the night'. Having steered John to the bathroom to use the 'loo and have a wash, I awaited my turn to perform the same ablutions. But a bellow suddenly came from behind the closed door: 'There's no bloody WATER!'

To rectify this oversight, I had to go back to No.6 and rouse Patricia who, fortunately, was still up talking with Danielle. This I had to do because only she knew where the stop-cock and the hot water system were controlled from at no. 4. Anyway, finally, this little glitch over, John and I settled in our respective beds. Though not before John had informed me that, as he hardly slept at night, he required a radio to listen to. A fact which explained why he carried a radio in his luggage, though not necessarily why it was such a huge 'ghetto-blaster'. Which instrument John insisted on having balanced on his chest throughout the night.

For a little while there was silence; and I began to drift off to sleep. But, The Mount being a seaside location, one hears seagulls – ours are noisy herring gulls – screeching in the night, as well as in daylight hours. Now, Heath-Stubbs being famous among contemporary poets for his ornithological knowledge – he had written many poems about birds – having asked me what the vague din (the windows being shut) was, I told him it was herring gulls, and this prompted a long dissertation on the sort of birds that frequent Notting Hill. Something I really needed to know at 2pm in the morning! Eventually, though, he lapsed into silence again. And I did drift off for a little while.

My next arousing came abruptly as the ghetto-blaster sprang deafeningly into life. Shouting non-poetically, 'DAMN-BLOODY-BLAST!' several times, John struggled to find the volume control switch, which he eventually did. Then he said, 'I hope I didn't wake you?' Adding, 'It doesn't normally give me any trouble.' speaking as he might of a wayward child or disobedient dog. 'No,' I lied, 'I wasn't asleep.' Out of the dark came the retort, 'Oh, good, you thought I might have been.' In silence I thought that not only had he disturbed me, but it was quite likely he had woken most of the people in The Mount for, as Patricia had often said, 'These houses were built without anticipating the advent of stereo sound.'

There then ensued a period of communing between John and his radio that was hardly *sotto voce*. A discourse which consisted on the one side of all bar the foulest Anglo-Saxon oaths, and on the other of knob-squeakings, half-sentences in various languages and crackling noises that sounded like bonfire burning sounds.

All of which manic struggle with a mechanical device ended when the radio slid off John's capacious chest and the bed onto an uncarpeted part of the floor. The enormous bang it seemed to me must inevitably reverberate through the walls of all the houses, most inevitably that of the elderly and somewhat unstable lady next door, whom we knew as the Black Widow until she gave up dyeing her hair jet. She was also a woman given to foully cursing at the top of her voice when watching football on TV. So I really did expect a ferocious banging on the parti-wall within seconds of the collision between the ghetto-blaster and the floorboards. Alternatively, or additionally, Patricia might come rushing round from No. 6 thinking John and I had fallen to fighting or throwing things at each other. 'Poets can be very touchy!', as she would say. But after about five minutes, none of those things having ensued, I concluded no one outside the bedroom had heard the bang; or, if they had, had chosen to ignore it.

There now ensued about a quarter of an hour's silence following on John's declining of my offer to retrieve the radio for him. 'Leave it where it is. I'm fed up with the bloody thing!' During this fifteen or so minutes of blissful silence I had just begun to drift sleep-wards again, when I heard a low muttering coming from my companion's direction. At first, I thought he was engaged in the proverbial 'counting of sheep'. Then I thought it was some sort of sleep mantra he was chanting to himself. Eventually, however, I could make it out. He was saying one word over and over: 'Boring, boring, *boring!*'

All hope of sleep being now lost for me, I decided to engage him in conversation. It seemed to me best to tell him about some of those writers, whose work he would know, who had lived and wrote in the locality of South Devon. A safe enough topic one would have thought?

'Robert Graves lived and worked in Galmpton for six years in the 1940's. Galmpton is a village about ten minutes in a car from The Mount...', I began, knowing that Graves had been an acquaintance and correspondent of Heath-Stubbs'.

'I thought he lived in Majorca?'

'He was driven out of Majorca by the onset of the Spanish Civil War; and after a couple of years spent in the States, he came here through his sister Rosalind, who was a GP in Teignmouth...'

'You know he was with that American woman in Majorca...what was her name? Changed it because she was a Jew; and with Hitler bellowing on the radio what he was going to do to the Jews, changing one's name was a sensible ploy.'

'Laura Riding. Her name was Laura Riding.'

'Yes, that was her name. She was a poet too. Better than Graves some think...'

'Especially herself. I wrote an obituary of Graves when he died, and got a furious letter from her saying she "had taught Graves all he knew about poetry". Which was a ridiculous assertion, I thought.'

'They had a difficult time together in Majorca. She tried to commit suicide by jumping out of an upstairs' window, and was only saved by landing in a hay cart that was passing at the time.'

In fact, the suicide attempt had taken place at a house in St. Peter's Square, Hammersmith. Laura Riding jumped to the ground from a third floor window and was severely injured. The police even interviewed Graves because there was a suggestion that Riding had been pushed out of the window. Nor, having visited Graves in Majorca, were there any hay fields or hay carts that I had seen, only miles of olive terraces. So Heath-Stubbs' anecdote was way off the mark. It, nevertheless, took me some while to not entirely convince him that his story was somewhat inaccurate. In the end, I decided to direct his attention to another literary local.

'Christopher Milne, the son of A.E. Milne ran the Harbour Bookshop at Dartmouth for many years until his recent death. He was the model for the Christopher Robin in Milne's children's tale.'

'Rubbish! That's impossible. The real Christopher Robin would have been too old.'

'Too old? Why do you say that?'

'Because the Pooh books date from the 1920's: Christopher Milne would have been a child then.'

'Exactly, and he's just died, so he can't have been more than in his late seventies.'

'Just died? How do you know it's the same Christopher Milne? Could have been a grandson, of course.'

'No, John, it was A.A. Milne's *son* – all the obituaries said so.'

'H'm, well, I'm surprised I must say.'

There was a longer silence while John digested this piece of literary gossip. I could almost hear him shaking his head in the darkness. In fact, as it was beginning to lighten outside, my friend's outline began to be visible. He was moving his head. When he next spoke, it was to inform me that he wished to visit the bathroom. Before Heath-Stubbs had slid himself even half-way along the single bed – a blind person's way of getting up, he claimed – I was up and out of the room to block his way down-stairs. The last thing I wanted was to see the local paper yelling in headline: FAMOUS POET FALLS DOWN BRIXHAM STAIRS. And, as with the Graves-Laura Riding suicide attempt, some bright reporter might have seen fit to add something like the following: 'Did he fall or was he pushed? Local poet, who had been sleeping with Mr Heath-Stubbs, questioned by police.'

Yes, indeed, all manner of misunderstandings could have arisen if our eminent poet visitor had crashed down the stairs in Tony and Fran's holiday home! But this did not happen, and later in the morning John and I were driven back to Totnes where, after morning coffee in the signal box there, which had been converted into a café, the blind bard was put on a train for London. John Heath-Stubbs , one of the most erudite and significant poets it has been my good fortune to know.

8.
THE SAFRANIERE

The *Safranière,* or the *Commune Libre du Safranière...*and yet more about Tony! Late one July evening in Antibes in the South of France – an evening so hot even the stars looked as though they were sweating. Fran, Patricia, Tony and myself attended a *fête de commune* called the *Safranière,* which means 'saffron plantation' for reasons not explained. It was a small, intimate annual fête held in a town square. A very local event, I don't think it encompassed much of Antibes: I got the impression that the particular commune it served covered only a small, but specific, district within the old town. It was presided over by a mayoral figure who was as jolly as an overweight sunbeam: a Frenchman given to smiling and shrugging alternately. He was probably not the Mayor of Antibes and Juan les Pins who occupies the Hotel de Ville, but some lesser dignitary. It was an occasion that consisted of dancing beneath palm trees between which were strung chains of lights; and the consuming of much wine and various cooked meats or cheeses on bread purchased from a variety of temporary stalls around the square. There were also more permanent cafés, shops and bars that opened onto the square. It was altogether a lively occasion; and one could feel that communal sense which the French seemed to have more successfully preserved than the over-consumerist Anglo-Saxons.

By an odd chance, when Tony and Fran had been looking to buy a property in Antibes, they had encountered a woman called Jackie who turned out to be an old school friend of Fran's. A tall, blonde woman in her middle years, Jackie had been a part of the British ex-pat community on the Côte d'Azur for some years. Anyway, she became instrumental in the acquisition of Tony and Fran's house in the old quarter of Antibes; and in introducing them to aspects of the local life such as the *Safranière.*

It was during our stay at the house in Impasse Sade, Antibes in July 2005 that there was a photograph in the local paper, the *Nice-Matin;* it showed Jackie as part of a group who ran the fête. In my notebook of the time I described Jackie as 'a statuesque blonde with a degree of insouciance and a touch of hauteur' – which is better than simply 'a middle-aged woman'.

When, a few years earlier we had first met her, Jackie was in process of acquiring a run-down villa with a view to doing it up so as she could move out of the town centre. And on the day of the *Safranière* we went back to see this hugely transformed dwelling with its blue crystal swimming pool, its terrace and acres of palm-lined garden. From the ruin we had first encountered, with its fetid, scum-green swimming pool and semi-jungle of out-of-control shrubbery, to the luxury villa in an impeccable landscape, the transformation was most impressive. But, already, Jackie was missing her immersion in town life and, within a further year, would move back into Old Antibes.

It was in a sort of sunken square or *place* just off the narrow road that runs along the ancient ramparts of the town where the fête was under way when we arrived. The varied lighting glittered and swung in the dark blue foam of night air, and music was belting out. I felt a bit, well, sad as I recognized much of the music spilling and blaring from loud-speakers in the mesh of trees was, to a Francophile like myself, inappropriate transatlantic pop. Still, after we had bought tumblers of wine from Jackie's stall, we went and joined her Swiss husband Peter and their wonderful dog, Freddie:

Teddy-bear-faced dog
Like a yapping rug –
Foolish sometimes
But, basically, no mug.

The only poem I've written to a real dog. Though, sadly, he is dead now.

Soon all of us were enjoying ourselves, despite the fact that I was compelled, nay, coerced into dancing several times. By then, it was approaching eleven o'clock of the evening; and with everyone happily tipsy – the four of us had already had a meal before getting to the *Safranière* – something amusing was bound to happen. And it did.

Tony had become aware – amidst the swirl of dancers – of a particular, somewhat provocatively-attired female. She was not over-young but was slender and moved effortlessly with an attractive showing of bosom. She appeared to be dancing alone. Except for occasionally when she was joined, briefly, by a strange-looking much older woman dressed like a Tyrolean mountaineer, a back-packer wearing heavy boots.

This latter fearsome creature was an elderly, muscular woman who was, according to the ever-informative Jackie, more of a man than a woman, 'if you know what I mean?' Tony and I supposed we did 'know what she meant'. But the mutual gyrations between the one Tony fancied and La Butch d'Antibes were but fleetingly *en passant*: there being no touching of bodies or holding of arms.

After a while, I realized that Tony – for whatever ambitions he may have harboured about being a Lothario wasn't one, so I volunteered to approach the lady in the skimpy dress ('no lady, a whore!', Jackie) and smooth the approaches, so to speak, when next she came twirling and gyrating in our general direction. My price for this act of charity towards my friend? A large glass of *vin rouge*. It was a price Tony thought worth paying. And when the opportunity duly presented itself, I sidled up to the woman in question and, after remarking favourably on her dancing skills, talked-up Tony's abilities in the same direction, telling her finally that 'mon ami' longed to partner her round the square. She seemed interested and, soon, they were dancing until the music for their first dance came to an end. And I was rewarded with my glass of wine.

When Tony rejoined me in the seating at the edge of the square, he made his best joke of the holiday. 'A poet, yes, William. But I've never thought of you as a pimp!' Before, however, he could resume dancing with the lady with the ample cleavage and the shimmeringly-short silk dress – and now on his own initiative – a man suddenly appeared at her side.

Her 'papa', or what? Her sugar daddy? Even – but surely not – her husband? We didn't know. But he looked distinctly of 'a Sicilian persuasion'. And as neither Tony nor I wished to end our wonderful holiday on adjacent slabs in the Antibes' mortuary, we abruptly ceased Tony's pursuit of the possibly attainable, and withdrew into safer company.

9.
MORE ABOUT TONY

Considering the fact that Brixham is not exactly 'on the beaten track', an extraordinary amount of socializing goes on at The Mount. Central to this gregariousness is Tony Morris, our outspoken friend. Mainly, Tony (and Fran his wife) live in a mini-mansion on Boar's Hill, Oxford. But they have two holiday homes: one in Antibes and one here in The Mount.

About five feet, eight inches tall, stocky, with not much hair left except a curly infringement like a silver laurel wreath on a large egg, with a decent beard trimmed close to his face. Until recently he wore spectacles, but doesn't anymore. His demeanour is that of a genial publican: a not inappropriate description given his frequent attendance at hostelries of welcome. He has a good business brain that errs, I think, on the side of caution: I do not think him too much of a calculated risk-taker. But it is Tony's sense of humour that runs in tandem with a permanent willingness to help others which most appeals.

As far as this humour goes, Tony is seldom a teller of crafted jokes, nor does he make many wisecracks. Rather is his a down-to-earth gift for introducing some, often lewd or outrageous, observation or tale into the conversation. He is one of those persons, like the jesters at royal courts of old, who can get away with the most startling of remarks even in the most refined company. It is not a gift that is easy to convey in writing, depending as it does on atmosphere and timing rather than wit. But at one particular weekend, to which I will devote this chapter, it began with a good example of what one might call a *tonyism.*

It was the evening prior to the sort of grandiose local event in which Patricia, myself and friends not infrequently get involved in Torbay…especially since the new millennium's Year of the Artist. Tony and Fran came to supper with us. Not having seen them for a chunk of time, there was some catching up to do. We brought them up-to-date on our activities; then Patricia asked Fran what had been happening on Boar's Hill or wherever. Hers was a sad tale involving the illness and death of a Danish lady called Aida, whom we had once met in Antibes. She had lived with her tax-exile husband on a yacht in the harbour at Antibes. Her husband was called Norman and he originally came from

Nottingham. It was a memorable meeting, being the sole occasion I've read poems on a millionaire's yacht: my usual scene being rooms above seedy pubs. Norman, a great toper, had resembled a giant bottle of *vin rouge* dressed in a smart blazer.

After Fran had finished talking; Tony had remained unusually silent. I asked him, 'So what's happened to you then, Tony?'

He looked at us mournfully, 'I've passed another of those milestones in life.'

'What do you mean?' I asked.

Solemnly he replied, 'I've discovered I'm *im-potent.*' He paused, before going into the matter in more graphic detail, 'I got the gin and tonic out and I tried to persuade Fran to put on frilly underwear...'

'I put on my leotard!,' she interjected indignantly.

'Can you imagine that? A bloody leotard! What good would that be for my libido? No good at all. I couldn't get going at all. And you can imagine what *that* meant for me? Your number one macho man. Now *im-potent!* ...So, like I say, I've passed another stage in life.' He finished on the same lugubrious note.

By now, of course, everyone at the table was convulsed with laughter. Very soon including Tony most of all: laughing to tears in the end. When a man can laugh so much at what many would regard as a personal misfortune, then clearly it can be seen that there is something out of the ordinary about Tony's sense of humour. The off-scourings of a generous nature probably.

As a further example of my friend's unusual sense of humour, I am reminded of another conversation: this time between Tony and what is termed 'a celebrity'. One of the few celebrities in this age of television firmly associated in the public's mind with Torquay. The conversation took place late one evening at the fourth Torbay Poetry Festival: another of those occasions that take up much administrative time at The Mount.

For the first time at the festival we had, as one of the events, a debate. The theme was: 'Actors read poetry better than poets'. Anyway, this put us in mind of the actress Prunella Scales whom Patricia and I had occasionally met. She it was, of course, whom the general public remember as Sybil in the sit-com *Fawlty Towers*, a Torquay Hotel. As an actress well-known for her love of poetry and for her role as Sybil Fawlty, it gave her a dual interest and relevance to the festival.

One of the centres of that year's festival where events took place was the Kistor Hotel. And, after the final event on the Sunday evening entitled 'Poems you thought you knew', which had been Prunella's performance, a number of us repaired to the hotel's bar. The bar itself was situated in one corner of a large room: the other and larger part of which was the ballroom. The dance floor was being used by groups of older men and women doing waltzes and foxtrots. At some point while we were in the bar, one of these senior citizen waltzers scuttled over to our group and asked Prunella, 'Are you Sybil out of Fawlty Towers?' Evidently quite used to such enquiries, Prunella smiled sweetly over her glass of white wine and agreed she was the very same. At which the older woman turned on her heel and, marching back to her companions, said triumphantly for all to hear, 'It is her. I told you it was!'

Prunella asked one of our group, 'Who are all those people dancing?' To which she received the answer, 'It's the SAGA crowd.'

'SAGA? What's that?'

At this Tony jumped in with, 'SAGA, you know, "Sex & Games for the Aged"!'

Without the least flicker of surprise, Prunella said, 'Really? How interesting.'

Emboldened Tony added, 'Of course, you see, being past the age of child-bearing they don't need condoms.'

'Really?' She self-echoed, 'No condoms? But…but what about disease?'

'Oh, my God!' exclaimed Tony, 'now you've ruined my holiday.'

Tony at his worst is usually socially at his best. Or if not his best, his most amusing.

But now let Tony slide, if not out of sight, into the background.

It is Easter Sunday 2005 and the culmination of many weeks' work by the curiously-named Torbay Arts' Base or TAB for short, an event that ran for a few years annually. Within the overall cultural framework of the bay – vaguely presided over by the local council – TAB was, in artspeak, an 'artist-led group', whose primary function was to liaise between the various art disciplines – painting, music, poetry and so on – within Torbay. It was a group of seven people including Patricia who joined it because she said: 'I'm determined literature shall not get overlooked.' The event of this evening was to be a kind of

Oscars' ceremony for the arts.

The chief driving force of the group was an actress (or one should now, in these gender-troubled times, say an actor) and theatre company director called Sarah Lincoln, the daughter of the recently deceased and much-respected local painter Tony Green. Both father and daughter possessed great energy and artistic goodwill. Tony Green founded the bay's major annual arts' festival, sadly dying during the period of the third festival. Sarah, who has great theatrical flair, decided to organize an awards' ceremony for the arts in memory of her father. The ceremony was held in a grand Victorian chocolate box edifice in Paignton called Oldway Mansion. It was formerly the home of the 19th century American billionaire Isaac Merritt Singer, the man who invented the Singer Sewing Machine. The place itself is a somewhat heavily vulgar mansion with an imitation Palladian façade stuck on the front, and much brownish marble within. Its main banqueting room is a pink and gold imitation of Versailles. Both the first and second generations of the Singer family lived there before it passed into the ownership of Torbay's civic authority. The first Mrs Singer was, interestingly, the sculptor's model for the Statue of Liberty; while her husband is best described as the Bill Gates of the 19th century. Numbers of Victorian and Edwardian celebrities like Lily Langtry and Isadora Duncan stayed at the place, and this seems to have led to its frequent subsequent use for movie-making. Such being the case, it was a most suitable setting for the TAB awards' ceremony.

Sarah, this whippet-thin young woman with close-cropped hair, whipped both the arts' group and her theatre company into line to assemble a stage with strobe lighting and huge TV screens to show the speakers, as well as laying on tables and catering for a hundred or so guests.

As the date for the ceremony drew ever closer, the organizing committee had more and more work to do. It was claimed that a thousand nominations for the awards had been received: voting forms having been in circulation since the previous December. The Torbay Arts' Base committee acted as self-appointed judges. In each category one could vote for an individual artist, for an artistic event which had taken place within the bay in the previous twelve months, or for an artistic organization.

After much fat-chewing, head-scratching and debate in committee, which seemed to go on for weeks, awards in all fourteen categories were decided upon. The literary award went to David Perman, an ex-BBC producer with an interest in church music, he had choreographed occasions in Torbay involving music, poetry and song; and had done it brilliantly.

Earlier, I mentioned the degree of socializing at our end of The Mount. It seems unending at times. The big day of the awards' ceremony found itself sandwiched between, first the supper had with Tony and Fran; then, on Easter Saturday, a drinks' party that turned into something more; and, on Easter Monday, a children's birthday party. The Saturday drinks' party turned into something more because our next-door neighbours, Neil and Shelley-Anne, came with a procession of relatives and kids (whom we'd not met before) each bearing edible gifts like they were a catering firm. Fran and Tony were also there for part of the time, before going off for another dinner appointment elsewhere. The presence of children somewhat curbed Tony's humorous sallies.

As is our wont, in between these bouts of conviviality, Patricia and I worked. She hardest of all, spending some part of each day preceding the awards' ceremony at committee meetings. Most of all spending nearly all Sunday, first at church, then at Oldway Mansion, only returning briefly in the late afternoon. Shortly afterwards it was off again to Oldway Mansion: all of us in Tony's estate car, with me lying horizontal in the rear where the dogs usually travelled.

A champagne reception preceded the awards and the dinner. The place was awash with painters, musicians, sculptors, digital imagists, ceramicists, and the usual sprinkling of arts' apparatchiks. As the evening progressed, it became clear that things, including a good quality dinner, had been well organized by Sarah and her cohorts: so well, in truth, that there is no need for tediously detailed description. The whole affair resulted in exactly the sort of awards' ceremony that only the deaf and blind could be unfamiliar with in our talent-crazy, TV-dominated era. Suffice it to say that, as an exercise in glittering vacuity, it was perfect. As for its value – if such things actually have any value – it lay in the fact that it constituted yet another, rather grander, symptom of cultural activity in an area (Torbay) which, until the arrival of the new millennium, was an undeniable cultural desert.

When David Perman ascended the podium to receive his award he took Fran with him, as one of his two collaborative sopranos in the Abide With Us church events he had organized, and he made a brief, courteous acceptance speech. At one of the two lecterns was a TV presenter called Jilly Parten; at the other the egregious Sarah: the former to announce each winner, the latter to give a brief judge's spiel about each category of award. The actual trophies were handed out by the sponsors of each event, and consisted of thick oblongs of clear, inscribed plastic like miniature gravestones, each with a pebble collected from a local beach stuck thereon. Not exactly your solid gold Oscar, but it was a start.

And that was really that. We diners received sweets and coffee, then went out of the banqueting hall to the bar. This was fine for a while, until a band, which went by the ridiculous name of 'Daddy Mango', began to raise the roof with its needlessly amplified din, and to which one was expected to dance. Only those old folk who had no idea they were old – or wouldn't admit it – and genuinely youthful guests, participated in this disco from hell. While in a corner, a friend and I speculated whether young people today were suffering from some kind of long-term aural stunning. I suggested that, in an age of wall-to-wall musak, sound had become a sort of drug which, like with hard drugs, one needed ever-increasing (i.e. louder) doses to maintain the thrill-level.

As was the case at the beginning of this chapter, so at its end I was to be found on the same table as Tony. Apart from Fran and David Perman, we also had a woman sculptor with us, plus the conductor of an orchestra and his wife. The artistic chat was so low-key however that Tony, apparently, did not feel further moved to shock anyone, oddly. But one final little anecdote to further illustrate Tony's especial verbal gift.

One year at the Torbay Poetry Festival I was talking with the poet Ian Caws from Sussex. For some reason I mentioned Tony. At first, Ian did not know to whom I referred. But a few further comments from me such as 'Tony's not a poet but, with his wife, an important patron of the festival.' Adding a further description or two to that and suddenly Ian exclaimed, 'Ah, yes, I remember him now!' And proceeded to tell how he had encountered Tony: 'I was at the bar buying a drink for the wife and myself. I think I mentioned to the barman that my wife wanted a different wine from mine, when this man waiting behind me in queue suddenly tapped me on the shoulder and said, "My wife has just been kidnapped by lesbians!" After having informed me of this fact, he fell silent. But what he'd said was the sort of remark one doesn't forget.'

That this was so, I agreed with Ian, and added 'the memorable utterance' was Tony's speciality…along with possessing a genius for DIY which ranged from installing fitted kitchens to repairing motor car engines. Also, like his wife he showed a truly Christian kindness to anyone in need…as well as a fine tolerance towards the many poets and eccentrics he encountered.

10.
JOURNEY TO VIENNA

Recently, we were in the gardens of Kenwood House in Hampstead when we received a phone call from our daughter and her husband – who were in Vienna, of all places. Barry was there on a business trip and Elizabeth had tagged along for the ride, so to speak. She'd heard how beautiful the city was from us and taken the opportunity to see for herself. It was the Sunday morning after Patricia's London birthday party (no numbers where females and their ages are concerned!) and their call reminded us of the time we went to Vienna in a minibus full of poets and academics: a vehicle belonging to a local Salzburg football team.

We had been in Salzburg, at the St. Rupert Conference Centre on the outskirts of that city for a three day symposium on contemporary British poetry. That conference had been the last official act before retirement in 1996 of the extraordinary Dr James Hogg, an ex-Carthusian monk, publisher and second-in-command at the *Institut für Anglistik und Amerikanistik,* or the English and American Literature Department of the University of Salzburg. A man who, through the Eighties and Nineties, was the facilitator of many interesting experiences for Patricia and me. It is possible that, but for James Hogg, we would never have visited Austria at all. But James made a lot of things possible for poets, with whom and their work he had a fascination. He was, in fact, a patron, very generous with his own money as well as that of the university. – It was also a coincidence that less than a fortnight after our daughter's phone call we were travelling again to Salzburg, this time to help present Dr Hogg with a *Festschrift* for his 80th birthday.

The 1996 conference was over and the gradual dispersal of the guest poets and jet-setting academics was under way. Everyone had given their papers on some aspect of the contemporary poetry scene – mine was on the long poem. Patricia's was all about running a literary magazine. I don't recall all the poets who attended: my friend Fred Beake and his great beard were there; the late John Gurney, an ex-fighter-pilot-turned-poet, who looked like an angel and had the ambition to 'write more verse plays than Shakespeare' was present; Joy Hendry, the editor of the Scottish literary magazine *Chapman,* swashbuckling lass of great intelligence had travelled to the conference; as had the late Jon Silkin, poet and editor, who told me, with a sort of odd confidentiality, that he saw himself as 'the Polite Man'; and, indeed, he seemed so. These were the persons whom Patricia and I saw most frequently at the gathering, along with Glyn Pursglove and his wife Parvin.

From the dawn of that last day, all lectures and events being finished, including the grand retirement party for Dr Hogg, most of us just sat around talking until it came time for us to depart as well. But Patricia and I weren't leaving Austria yet. We were going to Vienna the next day. Consequently, late that same afternoon she and I went walking along the banks of the Salzach River that cuts through the heart of Salzburg: a white snow-water river, swift over sharp and polished rocks, a watery turbulence under city bridges. On the way we met Jon Silkin, his beard and hair as hoary as St. Nicholas's: he was returning to the conference centre to catch a taxi to the airport. It was to prove the last time we would meet that tireless worker for the promotion of poetry – both his own and that of others. A few weeks later he was dead.

In the Marienplatz we were picked up by James Hogg's assistant (now successor) Wolfgang Görtschacher who, after collecting Tom Clyde, the Irish poet, drove us to the apartment where we spent the evening and night. I don't recall whether Wolfgang had the football club's minibus at this point. But the following day he certainly had, and Patricia, me, John Gurney, Dr Hogg, and Professor Anthony Johnson of the University of Pisa, were all travelling the road out of Salzburg in the direction of the Austrian capital.

It was to be a long journey. Our driver was an Austrian woman judge called Sonja, a bright, sharp, good-looking woman with short, dark hair. It transpired that she played tennis once a week with Wolfgang's ex-wife, Andrea, whom we had known formerly in both England and Austria. Doubtless the tennis game was an exercise in gossip as much as in keeping fit.

A considerable drive, many hours long into the gathering dusk. But after a beautiful journey through valleys and mountain passes, and the mysterious Vienna Woods, eventually we made the outskirts of Vienna. John Gurney, a great one for psychoanalysis, got very excited as we passed along the street where Freud had lived before the Second

World War. But our destination was not Freud's house but the romantic-sounding Radio Blue Danube. It was situated in a tall, stately building somewhat like the headquarters of the BBC in Portland Place, London.

For some reason that I no longer recall, I had been nominated by the good Dr Hogg to 'go on air' and talk about the modern long poem. I still have a tape of the radio interview. After the radio studio, the next place we went to in Vienna was the English Bookshop where we were shortly to give a poetry reading – at least Johnson, Gurney and myself were – and, in tandem with Joy Hendry, who was staying with friends in Vienna after the poetry conference, Patricia and she were to give brief talks about their magazines *Acumen* and *Chapman*. The shop's window was crammed with a display of our various publications which our presence was supposed to induce sales to a select audience of English-speaking Austrians. Whether we succeeded, I never found out.

While Görtschacher and Hogg were arranging matters in the bookshop, the rest of us managed to wander off to the nearby St. Stephen's Platz for a coffee and a look at St. Stephen's Cathedral. Judge Sonja guided us, taking us down many side streets, saying that to come upon an unexpected full view of the cathedral was the best approach. And she was right. Suddenly, rounding a corner, we came out onto the St.Stephen's Platz and there it breathtakingly was. An extraordinary edifice ('building' would be an inadequate word for it), with its silver swordfish-like steeple thrust floodlit into the night sky. Blue-lit and forming a tracery into the midnight blue sky – it caused both Patricia and me to stop and stare in wonderment. An indelible mental photograph. We even managed a quick look round the interior of the cathedral, but the altar space and a swathe of pews were barred off (literally) because an evening service was in progress. Priests in white vestments were censer-swinging by the light of hundreds of candles: a very impressive ceremony with Latin chanting and a great, sonorous organ booming away. Then again outdoors for a coffee at a pavement *konditori*, with the cathedral as a backdrop, made a perfect poetic start to the poetry evening ahead.

Later, back at the English Bookshop – which was modern and well-lighted, and quite indistinguishable from a thousand other bookshops back home in Britain or elsewhere – Patricia and Joy did their little double act about their respective magazines. They were preceded by a welcoming introduction given by Dr Hogg. James Hogg was one of those rare individuals whose nature somehow eccentrically runs against normality. A very shy man in private; and shy with people he knows; yet he always blossomed in public among strangers.

That part of the evening over – James's introduction and the talks by Patricia and Joy: such a contrasting pair, the latter tall and powerful-looking, Patricia more of an English-rose – it was the turn of the poets. Anthony Johnson read in his strong male voice full of hesitance, public school diffidence, and an acute awareness of the irony of words. John Gurney on a higher, more Blakean plane let his words fall down from the human stratosphere he carried within him: a sweet but serious voice. My turn was last, but I didn't mind that.

What I was soon to mind, however, was my sudden total inability to get my briefcase open in order to retrieve my poems from within. A couple of dozen pairs of eyes like round mocking jellies watched while I struggled to overcome the plastic intransigence of the special lock. Most embarrassing – the bloody thing just would not open! In the end, Wolfgang had the presence of mind to take one of my poetry books out of the window display, thus enabling me to give my quarter of an hour's reading. After this, the bookshop manager took us all to a local restaurant for a welcome meal. At the table, Wolfgang leaned across to me as I was in the act of pouring some much-needed wine from one of the carafes. 'That was a brilliant PR move!' he enthused. 'What was?' I demanded. 'Pretending you couldn't get your briefcase open, of course.' 'It wasn't a trick. Look, it still won't open!' I cried, handing it to Patricia who was seated next to me. I was determined to prove my point. With no difficulty whatever, she unlocked the briefcase. More than a faint smile hovered over Wolfgang's lips.

It was approaching midnight before we left Vienna – in my case full of red wine and *schnitzel* – and headed home to Salzburg. A few miles out of Vienna, Wolfgang suddenly grew agitated after hearing an announcement over the radio about 'ghost drivers' which, he explained, are a common feature of the *autobahns*. A ghost driver is a motorist who deliberately drives the wrong way along a motorway, whether out of a desire to commit suicide or for a 'dare' or some other mad reason. However, we met no ghosts, motorised or not, on that return journey.

It was another seemingly endless journey along unknown roads beneath starry skies and mountains. On arriving back in Salzburg, no matter the lateness of the hour, Wolfgang had promised himself, Sonja, and us a bottle of champagne.

After returning yet again to the St. Rupert Centre to drop John Gurney off and taking James home (we had left Anthony Johnson in Vienna to catch his middle-of-the-night train to Florence), we finally got back to the apartment. Undeterred by the fact we had all been away from our beds for the greater part of 24 hours; and that it was but an hour from dawn, with heads buzzing from lack of sleep and too many hours of driving, we nevertheless toasted the success of our journey to and from Vienna in glasses of good champagne. Which – I have to say – proved somewhat less of a 'lethal' experience than the dozen bottles of schnapps I, and the editor of the Northern Irish magazine *The Honest Ulsterman* Tom Clyde, had sampled the previous evening. Sonja's father owned a vineyard where this strong liqueur, so popular in Austria, was made in many varieties. She had prevailed on Tom and me to work our way glass by glass to oblivion…or almost. – The things one does for poetry? At least, that's always a poet's excuse, even if it impresses few people!

11.
A BIRTHDAY TREAT

And the things we do for our friends!

It was my friend John's birthday and his wife Gina wished to give him a special present for the occasion. Being American, there is often something a tad ambitious about the things she comes up with. For example, for his sixtieth birthday a year or two later than the time I am about to record, she had a miniature church organ built and installed in one of the drawing rooms of their house in Cheltenham…and all without his knowing of it in advance. It was, of course, constructed at the organ maker's premises and only installed the day before his birthday by simply arranging for John to be away in his London flat on the day in question.

John is a businessman, with a wide-ranging interest in classical music, especially church music of Bach, Handel and Hayden. The difficulty of buying birthday gifts for John is enshrined in the question, 'What do you buy for the guy who has everything?' John can drive cars; he has a pilot's licence; he can write his own computer programs; and he can play the piano, the harpsichord and the organ. John can do a whole heap of things, in fact, including making money. So what, I repeat, does one buy for such a guy? Well, Gina had another of her bright ideas. And as I was John's oldest friend I had to be involved in the surprise. And a real surprise it was to be, for I was not to be let into the secret in advance either; though Patricia was.

Come the day of the birthday, for a 'treat', rather than a physical present from Gina to John, the four of us set off in John's motor car around noon of a fine and idyllic day. Although John was driving, Gina was navigating, so he had no idea of our destination. A day deeply sunlit with a riot of flora along Cotswold verges. Apart from the slightly odd request from Gina to John and me to wear long trousers – no shorts – and heavy jerseys, inappropriately for such hot weather, there was nothing else to cause suspicion on that summer's day. Needless to say, however, careful observation will, sooner or later, arouse one's curiosity and speculative instinct. In the area of Chipping Norton I spotted notices that indicated we were heading to a place called Happy Valley and, within that nicely-named location, a farm.

Before we were quite at our destination, John had 'sussed out' what was 'in the wind', because he knew something of the place already. By the time we drove into a field set aside for parking at Happy Valley Farm I also knew what we had come for. And I didn't like the sound of it at all.

'A tiger experience?' I croaked, 'What's, er, that?'

'John gets to meet a tiger.' Gina informed me.

I looked at Patricia, 'Did you know about this?'

'I had to know to make sure I brought the right clothes for you.'

'The right clothes?' I whimpered, 'Can I stay and look after the car?'

'It's only a tiger cub.' said Gina soothingly. 'John's mad about cats, so I figured he'd just adore playing with a cub, okay?'

I have to say that I remained deeply skeptical of the value of this latest birthday present. Not because I denied John's love of felines, but because I saw no convincing reason why *I* should share this latest manifestation of his love for the creatures. I like cats too, but not enough to wish to meet every species of them in person.

But there was to be no escaping. We were ushered into an exceedingly crowded reception area – it was full of parents with kids desperate to meet goats, lambs, rabbits and guinea pigs: together with a lesser number there for what one might term the more 'cutting edge animal experience' (hence our heavy clothing.) The reception was adjacent to the farm's shop; and I heard Gina quietly saying to John, 'We could, of course, have had the wolf experience if you'd've preferred?' That sounded just as bad to me.

After Gina had paid for the pre-booked tickets – an act of expensive madness, I thought, like paying someone to break one's legs – we were told to sit down and wait for 'Kasmira's trainer'. It seemed the baby beast had a name. We had quite a long wait for the trainer until, John growing restive, observed, 'Maybe he's been eaten?' But the ladies studiously ignored the remark, Gina merely wondering how 'we're gonna recognize the guy with all these people around?' I suggested it would be easy, 'He'll probably be the one with scars on his face and deep scratches on his arms!'

My attempted humour was equally ignored until, a few minutes later, a young Australian in his late twenties appeared. He had some name like 'Terry'. Terry wore a dark navy, short-sleeved shirt with matching trousers: we all noticed immediately the abundance of scratches on his arms. I groaned inwardly. But there was nothing to do now but swallow hard and follow him.

The Australian took us into a huge barn partitioned up into stalls and animal pens populated with ponies, sheep, cows and goats; there were also smaller areas for rabbits, guinea pigs and lambs. It all very much resembled a sort of Heath-Robinson zoo. There was a circular space like they have in circuses; and a high-sided area which, when one entered it, was like a room without a ceiling. It had straw on the floor and two very low benches of the sort that might have been designed for small children. Terry apologized for the somewhat pungent aroma in the room, telling us they'd just conducted 'the wolf experience in here'. At one end of the room was a door identical to the one we had entered by, and which was firmly closed behind us now. Said the trainer, 'Please sit on the benches – Kasmira doesn't take to folk who tower over her.'

Since when have tiny tiger cubs, all full of playfulness like kittens, bothered about 'towering' humans? thought I, but said nothing.

Then the trainer went out of the other door leaving me at least in what is called 'an agony of suspense'. But it was not a suspense, only an agony, that lasted long. Though I tell an untruth really. For once I get caught up in the throes of the inevitable – like, for example, teetering towards the edges of 2000 feet precipices in the Himalayas in a Land Rover, or being shut in a room with a tiger cub that turns out to be considerably larger than a rotweiler – I grow unaccountably calm. Fatalistic.

Kasmira proved to be a six-month-old Bengal tiger. She had lived with Terry, her Aussie trainer, since a truly baby tiger cub, 'sleeping on my bed at night and going for morning walks over the local fields with my spaniel. She played beautifully with my dog. They both, in fact, slept together on my bed, until my spaniel began to suspect that Kassie was growing a bit big for him. Latterly, on our walks, I've had to put her on a lead...'

None of this impressed me. Asked Gina, 'May we stroke her – she looks adorable?'

By contrast, I asked, 'How long are we in here for?'

Replying to Gina's question only, Terry said, 'Sure, you can stroke her, but only on her back not her head. She doesn't like her head being touched.'

Even I stroked her, feeling that I had better do so in case she felt I was snubbing her. Her fur was harshly bristled as a doormat. Nor did Kasmira respond to our caresses in the usual feline way: Terry informing us that 'tigers don't purr'. Though subsequently I've read things about tigers that cast doubt on that piece of information.

Gradually, a sense of unreality descended on me; and while I can't say I enjoyed the experience, it 'had its moments'. For examples, Kasmira obligingly ('playfully' urged the Aussie) leaped up, put both her paws upon each of Terry's shoulders and seized his neck in her jaws. By taking something edible out of his trouser pocket and giving it her, he easily disengaged himself. Next, first on one bench then the other, the tiger sprang up and seated herself between Patricia and myself, then between John and Gina – quite undeterred by the well-known piece of advice, 'Never come between man and wife'. Thus seated in the exact posture of Bubastis, the great cat goddess of the Ancient Egyptians, and taller when seated than any of us, she was decidedly unnerving.

Tigers must have an instinctive knowledge of anatomy. In her most playful moods that dangerous afternoon, Kasmira seized first John, then me, by the leg, always close to the groin and thus near to one of the main arteries in the human body. Her playfulness was more alarming than painful ('She's very gentle', her trainer assured us), and, appropriately, she 'bit' the birthday boy three times to my twice. It was a sort of heavy gnawing at our thighs. In the bath that evening I was to discover my upper right leg was bruised purple; and likewise John discovered the same phenomenon. ('She's very gentle.')

For a brief moment, but only for a moment, Terry the Aussie absented himself from the cell-like room we were in – doubtless to generate yet a further *frisson* for his customers. Almost immediately – like she'd been trained to it – the tiger grabbed Gina's handbag. Then got hold of Patricia's too. While Kasmira was performing these antics I gazed longingly at the ten-foot-high wooden wall and wondered if there was any way I might vault it. But Terry returned abruptly with a piece of meat.

'She's snatched our handbags.' Gina to the trainer.

'You shouldn't have let her.' The trainer to both Gina and Patricia.

You could see what they were thinking. Something like: If you think we were going to try and stop a six-month-old Bengal tiger from...?

Terry flung the meat into the straw on the floor, 'You can stand up now. She won't bother you anymore.'

We watched as Kasmira licked and fondled the hunk of meat. As her trainer said, we were not worth bothering with anymore. And shortly afterwards we were released from that wooden cell...our 35 minute 'tiger experience' over. The release of adrenalin in the car as we headed back to Cheltenham was considerable and interesting.

'It was peculiar how Kasmira only went for women's handbags.' observed Patricia.

Said Gina, 'That farm was in the newspapers recently. A lynx had gotten out and wandered through the local village. It upset some of the villagers.'

'I expect the next thing we'll hear is the place has been closed down because Kasmira has eaten her trainer!' mused John.

I remained silent, merely taking the occasional deep breath.

It was John who was to be proved right. The animal farm in Happy Valley was shut down within a couple of years. As a public health hazard it was rumoured.

Now John is an accomplished musician but is not known for penning verses. However, when for my sixtieth birthday a festschrift was produced, John contributed a reminiscence of our long friendship. And he thought to include the following lines:

'Tiger, tiger, my, oh my!
Sank her teeth in William's thigh.
When she saw what she had done,
She sank them in the other one.

A heartfelt remembrance of the encounter with Kasmira the Cotswold tiger, and not an attempt to compete with William Blake's rather better-known 'Tyger, tyger, burning bright...etc.'

12.
BLACKMAILED INTO FAME

I am uncertain which of the two words 'blackmail' or 'fame' I should put in inverted commas here. No matter, neither are probably true as absolutes. Which is to say, they wear a touch of irony like dew on grass. For years – my family apart – my chief preoccupations, like those of Coleridge, have been the twin mysteries of poetry and metaphysics. The former is a struggling with words; the latter the challenge of real truth. Letting the poetry take care of itself for now, I will speak briefly of the latter.

'The major poetic idea in the world is, and has always been, God', said the American poet Wallace Stevens. Living in an ever-increasing secular society like the Britain of today, such a statement will come as a bit of a shock. But it is true. As with Socrates, so with me, I have spent much of my life trying to establish what is true. That, and writing poetry, have kept me out of any limelight in South Devon, where I live, or anywhere else. I should, however, mention that while I lived in creative exile in South Devon (Torbay to be exact), it was more a local exile in fact. For I had many friends whom I visited from time to time: but they were all in London or other parts of the Home Counties.

As the Millennium Year of AD.2000 approached, it was perfectly true to say that neither I, nor Patricia, had much of a social life in Torbay, despite having lived in the place for twenty-four years. In the interest of pursuing our joint and separate literary concerns, neither of us mixed in the local community; and certainly not in any literary life there may have been. The only writers we encountered were no closer to Torbay than Exeter; and my wife's chief cultural contact South West Arts in Exeter, who supported her magazine *Acumen* financially. Indeed, it was they – the West Country branch of the Arts Council of England – who brought an end to our, especially my, local exile. And it had to do with the Millennium celebrations. A government scheme to generate artistic celebration of that important date was launched.

The idea was to place 1000 artists – painters, musicians, poets, sculptors, etc. – throughout the U.K. in residencies with various organizations, areas, modes of transport and so forth. It was dubbed officially 'The Year of the Artist' and I was persuaded (kind of!) to become Poet-in-Residence for Torbay. This was achieved by a subtle combination of blandishments and threats imposed on me via Patricia: she a long-time client, as I say, of the Arts Council in the South West. As no applications (incredible as it might seem to anyone unaware of the culturally backward nature of Torbay) for any of these state-funded creative residencies were forthcoming from artists in Torbay, it was tactfully but firmly suggested to Patricia by one of the responsible art apparatchiks in Exeter that 'Your husband might like to apply?' It would be regarded officially as 'helpful' were I to apply to be Poet-in-Residence for Torbay in this special time. And this was how I was 'set up' for a bit of local fame and a lot of community involvement. Real life had caught up with me at last. For a year at least I would have 'almost a proper job', as my friend Tony said. Though not a job likely to make me a fortune.

As soon as it became known that Torbay had its first official laureate, various people started to contact me. Additionally, Torbay Council's principal arts' officer – one Alan Davies who claimed he had been a pub poet in the Sixties – he played a crucial part in my appointment, colluding, sorry, co-operating with South West Arts, and became an important conduit of information and facilitation for my job. Alan it was who provided the magical 'matching funding' required for all Arts Council grants. He also set up a committee whose multi-purpose nature was to coordinate my developing poetry programme with bodies like The Little Theatre and Torre Abbey in Torquay and the Palace Theatre in Paignton – all of which it was suggested I might like to use for any events I put on. I was also approached by several people, principally the curator of Torre Abbey, the house and museum situated at the back of the park on the Torquay seafront; next by John Miles, a leading actor at Torquay's Little Theatre, and a writer of humorous verses; then by Danny Pyle who ran the Torquay Writers' Group in Babbacombe-St. Marychurch. Danny was later to become one half of the Bay's amusing duo called The Two Fat Poets – his poetic companion or 'other fat half' being a retired publican called Les Jones: a versifier also, and with his ukulele a latter-day George Formby. The arrival of such new friends and acquaintances forced me to clarify my thinking and work out some sort of programme. So that when I went to address the Torquay Writers' Group one day in May 2000, I had cobbled together a rough outline of what I intended do.

My period of office, so to speak, was to run from 1st June 2000 to 31st May 2001. Sometime during those twelve months, fairly early on in fact, I had a minor brainwave. Knowing that, when my term of office was ended, I would be called on to write a report on my work, it occurred to me that I'd save myself a deal of effort if I produced a newsletter as I went along. The idea being to provide myself, as well as others, with a record of events and related matters, partly like I say to keep a record but, also, to help publicize the Year of the Artist in Torbay and, by producing the newsletter in hundreds of copies for distribution around the bay, give a sense of cultural and poetic quickening in the local community. A kind of pre-blog blog!

In the end, this newsletter – which I entitled *The Residency,* and which appeared twice annually – became a sort of mini-newspaper reflecting those events I organized around the district; as well as other things that sprang up as spin-off from this Year of the Artist. Like Dr Johnson with *The Rambler,* or my friend the late Peter Russell with his newsletter *Marginalia,* I wrote most of the various reports of events. There was no one else to do it, apart from Patricia who did one or two bits of journalism for it; but I signed my various pieces under different initials to lessen the appearance of egotism; and, also, because I was, from time to time, forced to include myself in the various narratives. But rather than trust to memory, or allow myself the privilege of later 'creativity', here are some of the articles from

THE RESIDENCY – a musepaper

Interviewed on BBC Radio Devon at the start of his residency, William Oxley confessed that, like so many Year of the Artist appointees, he felt himself entering somewhat uncharted territory. "After 25 years as a private poet, suddenly I find myself asked to be a public poet ... But at least, it's an opportunity, not too often given to poets, to put something back into the community." Asked what he felt he could give to the community of Torbay and how the job had come to him, he replied, "There is an old Chinese proverb that runs something like this: If you have a penny, spend a halfpenny on bread so that you may live, and a halfpenny on a flower so that you may have a reason to live. In my case substitute poetry for flower and what we are talking about is the quality of life. All the arts contribute to the quality of life – help provide the reason for living – hence the idea behind this national scheme called The Year of the Artist, of which my bit is being poet-in-residence in Torbay for one year. I have, of course, lived here for many years and been *de facto* poet-in-residence, which is maybe why I was chosen in the first place. The powers-that-be who determine such things looked around Torbay and said, "Hey, there's a poet living there – we'll have him!"

I think, too, that when the Rockingham Press, which is a well-known poetry publisher in the Home Counties, published my autobiography, called *No Accounting For Paradise*, last year and it contains a fair amount about my life in Torbay, that, too, may have had something to do with the appointment.

The sort of things I intend doing during the next twelve months include setting up various poetry events culminating in a Torbay Weekend Poetry Festival. Then running a national poetry competition to put Torbay on the wider Literary Map, visiting schools, old people's homes, etc., and distributing free a range of posters containing poems, past and present, written about Devon and, especially, Torbay. You see, tens of thousands of people come to Torbay every year. And why do they come? They come to find their little bit of paradise for a while. It is beautiful and, therefore, poetic. It is to the credit of Torbay Council, South West Arts and the National Lottery people, that they have decided to capitalize on this fact, and realize something of the cultural dynamism of the place. Hitherto, only the local poets and myself have really sought to express this poetic quality – which is, as much as the sea and the kind climate and the good commercial facilities, a sort of spiritual truth or experience. Me, and the other poets around, are here to articulate this fact.'"

THE POET-IN-RESIDENCE'S THINKING ...

It was a daunting task to be asked to be Poet-in-Residence for Torbay. How does one go about raising the awareness of poetry in any area? Though I've lived here for nearly twenty five years, I wasn't sure how many people were actually interested in poetry, or could be encouraged to be interested. Firstly, I thought of actually reminding the people of Torbay about poetry and to this end I organized a series of free poetry posters which I tried to get into many places at the start of my residency. This in itself was quite funny as several shop-keepers were very suspicious and thought I was trying to sell them something. Then we came to the events. Now among poets I am known to have something of a philosophical disposition. This informs my thinking on everything. So, in organizing poetry readings for Torbay, I aimed for more than the conventional event of an invited guest reader addressing an audience. It seemed to me, from the very beginning of my residency, I had to both stimulate and involve that part of the community likely to develop an interest in poetry. Stimulate by bringing together a couple of guest readers who would not only provide a contrast in work styles but, also, would somehow suggest a way in which poetry itself related to other art forms or to some other ambience than of, say, Torbay alone. This is why I had a poet and trumpeter on the same bill; and why I presented two poets from London who had both visited Torbay before and written about the place. And, at every event, I involved the local poetry community by inviting any member of the audience who wished to read a poem of their own or just recite a favourite poem by a favourite poet of theirs.

THEY CAME, THEY WROTE, THEY RETURNED

For years, publisher-poet David Perman and doctor-poet Danielle Hope have been coming to Torbay. Two poets, familiar figures on the metropolitan literary circuit, who appreciate Torbay a great deal and, like the Poet-in-Residence himself, discovered poetry in the place. One of Danielle's best known poems celebrates `The Hog's Back' – that headland at Churston Cove, Brixham. Here it is in all its direct simplicity:

HEADLAND AT HOG'S BACK
   (Churston Cove)

We climb to the top. Lichen

straddles odd white rocks,
butterflies glitter, water claps.
Our ankles are torn with broom.

Headland. It sits like a decision.
Green in summer, exact in winter
when storms roar and the cove wails
under the beat of sea upon stone.

So theirs was the pioneer event of the residency, and it took place on a warm June evening in the welcoming intimacy of the Palace Theatre bar at Paignton. It was anticipated that this event would not fill the theatre – and it didn't – but glasses were rapidly filled and emptied and, probably for the first time ever, gallons of verse and poetry were spilled about the place. Members of the public numbered fewer than ten, yet those who came not only showed a lively interest in poetry – providing an attentive audience for the guest readers – but some read poems of their own. Les Jones, better known as "The Bard of Babbacombe", and his friend Danny Pyle, the organizational lynch pin of the Torbay Writers Group, came along to see how the Poet-in-Residence managed things, as did other members of the local literati. And while "bums on seats" were fewer than could have been desired, the evident enjoyment of all present was manifest: an enjoyment underpinned by some lively and serious questioning of the guest poets at the end of the evening.

Said an official of Torbay Council a few days afterwards, "I hear that the audience for the first event was small, but the bar takings were up considerably". "That's poets for you!" replied the Poet-in--Residence ... and he should know!

TRUMPETING POETRY

Known to many poets both in Brixham and London for her culinary skills as a literary hostess, Patricia Oxley decided to turn her husband's second poetry event into a day-long social occasion. As a client of South West Arts, who support her literary magazine *Acumen*, she has also an official role in the Year of the Artist residency. So before the next event which took place in the Coffee Lounge at the Brixham Theatre, Patricia laid on a splendid buffet for around fifteen people, including the two "stars" of the occasion. The proceedings both before and after the poetry reading were especially enlivened by the presence of Les Jones, the Bard of Babbacombe, who not only writes poems, but sings his songs to the accompaniment of a ukulele – as well as enjoying himself by sketching people. And sketching people was what he indulged in throughout the proceedings. The reading, subtitled "an afternoon with a difference", was helpfully advertised the day before in *The Brixham News*, but what that paper didn't say, and couldn't, was that the audience – though still small but creeping up from 8 to 14 by now – proved also an interesting "mix". For the first time holiday-makers were attracted to an event, including a couple from a Sussex village much in the news just then through the brutal murder of a little girl. But at least, it showed that people came from all over the place to Torbay and that poetry, in this case poetry and music, can provide an additional attraction. Whilst just to make a further point about the strange power of poetry, other members of the audience included a well-known local postman, a couple of jazz fans from Oxford and a five-year-old girl who came to recite a poem (which recitation earned her the loudest clap of the afternoon).

As for the main performers, Stuart Flynn, an Australian lawyer working in the City of London, is an accomplished poet and trumpeter with over 500 tunes in his head, many of which are classical pieces. And Alexis Lykiard, novelist, essayist, poet, jazz and cricket enthusiast, is a writer of great experience. Both acquitted themselves well, opening pathways between different media as the Poet-in-Residence wished!

THE TWO FAT POETS

Advertised as "an entertainment" at the St Marychurch Precinct Centre ("Through the lych gate opposite The Snooty Fox"), and at which "The Poet-in-Residence for Torbay William Oxley, will preside", this was the brainchild of Les Jones and Danny Pyle, the two chief male pillars of the Torbay Writers' Group.

Introduced by the Poet--in-Residence as "Poetry's answer to Weightwatchers", the two performers created a lively occasion, only slightly hindered by Les's "Heath-Robinson" mechanical word-scroller (made from a disguised Black and Decker drill and several rolls of paper and tubing) which was to enable the audience to sing-along with the choruses of some of his ballads like `The Internet Blues' and `The Man They Could Not Hang'. The Two Fat Poets suggested that, as the Bay now had its "own laureate" and that "poetry was really taking off", they could help move things forward by organizing their own "gigs": and if this first one was anything to go by they will prove a welcome addition to "the cause".

"GOT TO GET THE HAY IN, SEE!"
POETRY AND SONG

In the rehearsal room of the Little Theatre on a bright August afternoon, the Poet-in-Residence told a much-increased audience that "Another way into poetry is by examining its relationship with song." He quoted the early English composer William Byrd (1543-1623), "there is not any musical instrument comparable to the human voice". He then went on to mention how the great folk musicologist Cecil Sharpe told that the singers, from whom he collected melodies, had great difficulty remembering a tune if they could not "also recall the words." In addition, Oxley wished to emphasize the aspect of poetry as a performance art and so this event had been advertised as presenting the work of "Three talented wordsmiths who make performance poetry respectable". Paul Cowlan, a Devon man long-based in Germany but who was fortunately doing a current UK tour, was on hand to provide witty and intelligent songs – as well as straight poems. Swansea-based Christopher Smith, an academic and an authority on the Romantic poet Robert Southey, gave an amusing and thoughtful reading in his inimitable and insouciant manner. While John Miles, Torbay poet and actor from the Little Theatre, gave a sometimes passionate, sometimes witty reading of his own work. And, once more, a number of poets from the audience came forward to "strut their stuff" or just recite it in quiet, sincere tones. Then just to show that Oxley didn't actually have to import singers from abroad to emphasize the relationship between poetry and song, once more the Bard of Babbacombe was on hand to give a ballad or two of his own. The sizeable audience was a clear testimony to increasing interest being taken in the work of the Residency. As one member of the audience, a farmer, said, apologizing for leaving at the interval, "This is the first poetry-reading I've ever been to. Sorry I can't stay for the second half, but I've got to get the hay in, see?"

VOICES IN THE GALLERY

Historic and beautiful Torre Abbey was the perfect setting for an event relating poetry to paintings. During the 20th century more poets than ever before have written poems about particular paintings. The renowned poet and doctor of medicine, Dannie Abse, together with his wife Joan, an art historian and a leading authority on the Victorian writer and art critic, John Ruskin, have developed this unique talk which involves slides of famous paintings like Braque's `Standing Female Nude' and Paulo Uccello's `St. George and the Dragon' together with poems inspired by the paintings. Altogether the show involved a dozen famous paintings with poems by such writers as W B. Yeats, Ezra Pound, Wallace Stevens, W H. Auden and Carol Ann Duffy, and the long upper gallery of Torre Abbey, with its fine antique furnishings and paintings, provided a superb venue. When Joan Abse had finished her talk and their joint readings of the poems, after a suitable interval, Dannie Abse gave a fine reading of some of his best known poems like the chillingly sad `In The Theatre' about a man who died as a result of a brain operation, and the delightful, much anthologized poem `Not Adelstrop'.

The audience responded with great enthusiasm to everything and, had it not been for the current fuel crisis affecting travelling, this event would have attracted the biggest audience yet – as, it was, around forty people turned up, and many apologies for absence were received by the Poet-in-Residence.

WOMEN IN POETRY

Turning every which way ... as Americans, if not Torbay's laureate, might put it, there has been "a consistent attempt by me to present poetry from as many angles as I can think of", Oxley informed the small but appreciative audience in Paignton's Princess Theatre bar. Yes, an appreciative audience – with even the barman showing a rapt interest in the proceedings. This time the event was angled towards what is probably the greatest seismic shift in poetry in modern times: the invasion of Parnassus by Amazonia. The two representative Amazons, – though Amazons by gender and not by appearance – were National Poetry Competition prize-winner Caroline Carver and Ann Gray, author of a well-received book of mythological re-creations. Caroline, who spent a vividly recollected childhood in Jamaica living on an old slave plantation, regaled the audience with those memories written in a West Indian patois; while Ann read love poems and others that retold, in a modern idiom, Celtic tales. Both poets, long-time residents of Cornwall and active in West Country literary life, were happy to share their poems and their experiences as women poets in a world until recently dominated by men; a phenomenon discussed lengthily and intelligently between audience and poets after the reading.

TEACHING POETRY

Against a lively background of cafe-clatter and clutter, and whisper of ruminating sea through half open windows, before a panoramic vista of the whole of Torbay via picture windows filling alternately with sunlight and cloud-grey shadow, two more visitors to the Bay imparted their love of poetry. Love of poetry is the essence of teaching it. Not accepting *poeta nascitur non fit,* Ben Jonson averred that poets "are born *and* made". So Glyn Pursglove, not a practising poet but a university lecturer in the subject, got together with the elegant Rose Flint, a poet and creative-writing tutor to tell us how it might be taught. Both showed their deep experience of the subject to an intimate audience of local poetry *afficianados.* Which, referring to Ben Jonson again, is a better word (albeit it Spanish of whom the Elizabethans didn't approve: locking a number of them up in Torbay's Spanish Barn after the defeat of the Armada in AD1588) than his invented word "poetaster". Each spoke and read for a half hour in a flawlessly professional style which proved both thought-provoking and question-drawing. Glyn stated that much could be learned about the art of poetry by studying bad verse (whether deliberately bad as when Shakespeare uses such for the "mechanicals" in *A Midsummer Night's Dream,* or innocently as in some poems by well-received authors who were apparently having an "off day"). He then went on to recite some "bad" verse, much to the delight of the audience.

Rose illustrated her talk with her own work, a delicate flowing of imagery and craft so well fused together that one local poet was heard to say afterwards, "After listening to that should I really bother to write my own?

Such were some of the events organized to promote poetry in Torbay. Other things included visits to schools to bring poetry to children; visits to introduce disabled people to poetry; and events to demonstrate the importance of a readership, plus a final summary of the poet-in-residence's findings about responses to poetry:

'THE NATURAL AUDIENCE FOR POETRY'

Carrying out this residency to the best of my ability during the Year-of-the-Artist has been both a pleasurable and a revealing experience. The most difficult aspect of taking poetry out of the classroom, out of academia and the closed world of Contemporary Parnassus generally, has revealed a number of things, two of which particularly stand out.

Between the specialized, even élite, world of modern poetry, and what I would term "the Natural Audience for Poetry", there exists a seemingly fixed gulf and my experiences in Torbay and elsewhere have only served to confirm its existence. This audience, a somewhat heterogeneous section of the community is united, as far as poetry is concerned, by little save a natural, if often poorly informed, taste for poetry. It is a non-expert, fairly innocent and, therefore, kind of "pure" taste for poetry: an unaffected interest whether the parties concerned are simply readers of poetry, writers of it, or both. And one other thing characterizes this ill-defined but natural audience for poetry and which can also be said to unite it – and that is an aversion to what is all-too-loosely termed "modern poetry". By this latter, vague notion, it seems is meant the higher-profile, fashionably canonical work that journalists, critics, publishers, etc., have been pushing for most of the last century. It is an aversion which many living and practicing poets encounter in two ways. Firstly they encounter it critically; in the rigid distinction that this natural audience for poetry frequently insists on (at poetry readings, for example) between prose and poetry. Speaking for them for a moment, what they mean is that they recognize the difference between prose and metrical verse, and will only admit that poetry can be associated with the latter. In other words, for them free verse is never anything but chopped-up prose and, as such, not poetry at all.

The second contributory factor to this aversion lies in the fact that much of the natural audience for poetry – which is made up of non-writers of verse plus legions of amateur poets – "amateur" in the best sense – do not admire poems for craft or technique but simply for their ideas or sentiment.

It is in trying to bridge this gulf that I, like all modern poets, face the greatest challenge. Many poets, of course, don't bother, but simply get on writing their poems and hope the problem will go away. But if I was to do the job I was given in this Millennium Year-of the-Artist, I was obliged at least to try and meet the difficulty. And the only way I could hope to do it was by exposing "the two sides" to each other, thus bringing them together, however temporarily. Thus it is that this, and the previous issue of *The Residency*, constitutes a record of my various attempts. For reasons of cost, and because of the fact – also discovered during my work in Torbay – that the more high-profile names of contemporary poetry are completely unknown to the wider world, even to the wider "natural audience for poetry", I chose, for many of my events, lesser known but still highly competent practitioners of the art of contemporary poetry.

It will be appreciated that – apart from my final summing up on the natural audience for poetry – the little verbal cameos in *The Residency* rise no higher than their equivalent in any church magazine. But they do show how relatively easily I moved outwards from the quiet creative life – almost a hermit's life in Torbay – to something more communal. From the contemplative to the active life, in fact.

13.
THE UNFORGETTABLE TORRIANO

The more poetry readings one gives, the more the anecdotes proliferate. This is because such occasions are happenings that are adjuncts to the imaginative life, and the fancy cannot help intruding and, not infrequently, running riot on such occasions. I often think some student should write a thesis on poetry readings. If he or she did, one of the first things they would encounter, as evidence of the poet's vanity, would be the concern for audience size. I have often talked this over with fellow poets and, on one such occasion, recall masochistically boasting to another poet about a reading I gave in Luton years ago to "An audience of 2 – surely the record?"

But my companion was able to cap that with an, admittedly, apocryphal story involving the poet Roy Fuller (a later version gave it as Roy Fisher) who was invited to give a reading somewhere in Lincolnshire. The venue, it seemed, was a barn that had been converted into a local arts' centre and it was situated well off "the beaten track". To compound the poet's difficulties of getting to the venue was not only the remote location but also the appalling weather – it happened to be the middle of winter. But, again, such is the vanity of poets (doubtless they would read in Hell if invited) that the poet in question overcame every obstacle and arrived in time.

Unfortunately, the audience did not: there being only the organizer and his wife present at the magical hour of 8 p.m., when the reading was supposed to start. "Never mind," said the organizer with all the usual optimism poets encounter on such occasions, "people don't usually arrive on time we find . . . we'll give it another quarter of an hour." Well, of course the poet did "mind" because – as is also the way with these things – not only was there no audience in evidence, but there was no sign of the promised (by telephone) "beer and sandwiches": and he had come all the way from London "on a filthy night". By 8.30 p.m. there was still no sign of any audience; so the organizer informed the poet that "my wife and I will read in the first half – we're poets, you know?" Of course, the poet hadn't known any such thing – but he went along with the suggestion because, naturally, "it gave more time still for the promised audience to arrive". Well, the organizer and his wife droned on until 9.30 p.m., then gave up, saying: "We usually have an interval of ten minutes before the guest poet reads. . ." There was still no audience; and the poet could see, at last, the organisers were beginning to show anxiety, as he thought on *his* behalf.

But not at bit of it. Said the organizer, handing the poet a small brown crumpled envelope: "Here's your fee. Someone may still turn up, of course. But, unfortunately, my wife and I have to leave now. When you have finished your reading would you mind switching the lights out, locking up, and handing in the key at the house opposite." – So that was, my companion assured me, the record for the lowest attendance at a poetry reading: *"Minus two!"*

It is true that lack of audience has never been the problem at the readings at the Meeting House in Torriano Avenue, London NW5: there has always been the National Average Audience for Poetry Readings (i.e. 15) present and, on the many occasions I have been there the audience has ranged between 30 and 40 people. Rather it is the idiosyncratic and, sometimes, less-than-credible touches given to the events at Torriano that can be a problem. It is as if this uniquely homely venue run by John Rety and Susan Johns, with assistance from their daughter the artist Emily Johns, was simultaneously helped and hindered by the presence of the Muse.

Nowhere I have ever read have things ever gone so well for poetry, or been liable to go off-course so abruptly. The first time I went there was at the invitation of Dannie Abse who was the evening's guest reader; and I'd asked him what the place was like. "Well. . ." he said carefully "it's kind of special – especially unpredictable." And he'd told me how, the first time he'd read there, he'd scarcely got into his stride when a furious row had broken out in an adjacent room, and he'd eventually had to stop reading because "the quarrel was actually more interesting than what I was reading!"

True to form, that evening I first went with my friend, Dannie's reading was again interrupted – twice. The first time by a man who suddenly rushed from the premises shouting: "I didn't come here to listen to other people read their poems, only to read my own!" (Probably, sadly, one of the most honest utterances ever heard at a poetry reading.) And, on the second occasion, a female member of the audience, also a well-known poet, suddenly leaped up and cried, "Can you stop? I must have a pee!", and, forthwith, clambered over the rostrum on which the guest poet was seated, and disappeared through a door at the rear which led to the toilet. The audience remained silent, and the only sounds moments after were the flushing of the toilet and the clattering back up the short flight of stairs leading to the rear of the podium.

The poetry readings are almost always on a Sunday evening, and in the first half of the event are 'readers from the floor'. Naturally, such readings are of variable quality: there being about a dozen and a half poets volunteering samples of their work. And over the years I have attended the Torriano readings there has been the occasional singer too: none more memorable than Walt. Who he? Dare I say that Walt was a purveyor of political protest songs, very much in the style of the 1960's. If there was a Society for Vocally Challenged Nightingales, Walt would be president thereof. There were other politically radical singers, too, like Eric, another regular. But having poor expertise in singing myself, I will turn back to the matter of poetry itself.

Torriano – which in my poem 'Poetry Reading, NW5' I liken to a scout hut – is a long narrow room with a door leading onto the street and a small stage at the rear. And the matter of the dog and my first solo reading is what I now recall. I recall the dog – a big black hound – first, and the image of it preventing Stephen Spender getting to the stage at Torriano one crowded evening. The place was packed and Spender, who was guest reader, was late; he had great difficulty making his way down the narrow room; and for an eighty year old veteran poet to make his way unsteadily through the friendly throng only to be confronted by an unappreciative mastiff was, well, disconcerting.

Equally disconcerting for me was to find myself confronted with this same creature when, a couple of weeks later, I was the evening's guest reader. And, while speaking of things disconcerting, as well as of audience numbers, I should begin by saying that the audience that evening was "three times the national average" – i.e. around 45... which was regarded as very good. I should also repeat that the programme of an evening at Torriano always follows the same pattern of readers from the floor in the first half, then a short interval, followed by, in the second half, the guest reader. Which can, of course, mean that the guest reader has to sit through a deal of lucubrations, some very indifferent, from members of the audience – though it is a small price to pay for their "half hour of glory" most guest poets think. While none, I guess, noticing those poems from members of the audience that are clearly better than their own.

I must say, though, I found myself somewhat disquieted when, at the interval of that first reading by myself, Mine Host John Rety stood up and said: "If anyone wants to get a drink, there's an off-licence just round the corner", and the entire audience upped and left. I had visions of reading – as at Luton – to the organizer and his wife plus one other, my own wife. But not so, gradually the missing audience began to trickle back and take their seats, fortified with cans of lager and bottles of plonk.

But the Hound of Hell (and his owner, a semi-inebriated man in a long raincoat and sporting a red Egyptian fez) was still there. As I began my reading, the dog started to walk up and down in front of the small stage like it was a guard dog, and I was something to be guarded. . . which I suppose was a slight improvement on the attitude it had seemed to evince towards Stephen Spender. Unfortunately, however, and I should have explained this before, the said dog had its right back leg in plaster of Paris, having broken it in the fortnight since the Spender reading. Furthermore, the floor at Torriano was uncarpeted. With the result that, throughout my reading, I had to endure this dog pacing up and down below me – pad, pad, pad, clump, pad, pad, pad, clump – and not always in time to the numbers I was lisping.

Things achieved under adversity are often the most successful; and, strange as it may seem, that was the best and most enjoyable reading I ever gave at Torriano. And despite its having been dogged – sorry for the pun – by certain anxiety-making features, several people came up to me afterwards and spoke warmly of my reading, including the man in the red fez who said: 'Best bloody poetry I've heard in weeks!' Modesty, of course, prevented me from contradicting him ... and I even stroked his dog, if only in the interests of free verse.

Mention of the man in the fez, reminds me of another incident. For many years Camden Council subsidized the Torriano Meeting House for all the good work Rety and his wife Susan did for the art of poetry. But there came one year when the local council decided to stop the grant. There was a great outcry about this, including much publicity in local newspapers such as *The Hampstead and Highgate Express,* which culminated in a heated meeting between the leisure and entertainments' committee of Camden Council: Torriano was represented by John Rety, Dinah Livingstone, Arthur Jacobs and several other interested parties including the aforementioned Fez Man.

At first, the representatives of the Council were adamant in their refusal to continue the subsidy. But, it appears that at this meeting, the fez-wearing poetry lover (who may well have been an Egyptian for all I knew) turned up with a ceremonial sword which he unsheathed and waved at the Council representatives – to the latter's great consternation and terror. But, whatever, it did the trick and no further attempts were made to withdraw Torriano's grant.

Some months later I asked John Rety what had happened to the knight in shining plastic mac, whom I hadn't seen from the day Torriano began charging an entrance fee to get into events — something Camden Council finally insisted on. Rety shook his head sadly and said, 'He got burnt to death in his flat, poor man'!

For a while an Australian lawyer came into our life following a reading I gave with Dannie Abse, Mimi Khalvati and others at the Barbican Library in London. His name was Stuart Flynn and he had an Italian wife called Claudia, who was a film maker. Stuart had pretensions to being a poet and was a teetotaler like Shelley. One Sunday he and I were joint guest readers at Torriano and Claudia filmed us. He read first with a professional efficiency, probably due to his legal background; and as his other talent was that of trumpeter, he gave the audience a tune or three. And his wife filmed the proceedings.

Unfortunately, as the CD film shows, I clambered up onto the stage looking rather like a drunken caricature of Winston Churchill. Having been wined and dined at a local hostelry to celebrate Stuart and Claudia's 1st wedding anniversary, I was somewhat the worse for wear. When I stood to read I swayed visibly. But oddly, I had scarcely got through a couple of poems when my instability and swaying vanished, and I acquitted myself commendably...even my principal critic Patricia thought so. As for myself, I took it as a small empirical proof of what was frequently said of Dylan Thomas, namely, that as soon as he began reciting his poems he sobered up.

Many interesting anecdotes accrued to me of Torriano events I had attended and stories told to me of occasions I was not at. Equally,

I met many interesting poets, poetasters and other *literati*...as well as artists and printmakers. One such was the ever-cheerful Emily Johns, the daughter of Susan Johns and John Rety. Emily illustrated my only published children's book *Firework Planet* and I acquired a painting of hers which greatly intrigued me. As Patricia and I had involvement with Nepal and Emily was married to a Nepali, with whom she had a son, we conveyed some of the child's drawings to its grandmother in far off Kathmandu. While, in due course, Emily also illustrated my book of poems about Nepal which was published by Hearing Eye. And right from the inception of the Hearing Eye publishers, which also operates from the Torriano Meeting House and was founded by John and Susan, Emily has designed each book or pamphlet of poetry published there.

Over the years from Hearing Eye's first publications, those of John Heath-Stubbs, Arthur Jacobs, Adam Johnson and Rety himself, the press has established a breathtaking list of contemporary poets such as Dannie Abse, Peter Philips, Leah Fritz, Maggie Butt, Timothy Adès, Paul Birtill, Brian Docherty, Kathleen McPhilemy, Mario Petrucci, and many, many more. But for a further insight into the many-sided John Rety who, with his partner Susan Johns, founded this remarkable press as an offshoot of the Torriano reading venue, see the later chapter in this book, 'The Chessman Cometh'.

14.
ABSENTEE LANDLADY

Flynn the Irishman was talkative, friendly, came from Dublin, and was a Sufi. 'Personable' is the word for him on account of his friendliness and exceptional good looks.

I never got to the bottom of the Sufi business, for he would fend off my tentative nosiness with quotes from someone he referred to as 'Rummy' – whom in my more enlightened years I now know was the great Sufi poet-philosopher Rumi, or Jalalu'l-Din Rumi to give him his full title. It did, however, have something to do with why he was, if not modest for an Irishman, at least moderate; as well as open-hearted. I also think he was honest, despite the fact he borrowed small sums of money from me without ever paying them back as he was often strapped for cash, was always waiting for cheques that never seemed to come.

There is a respectable, unquiet road in Cricklewood, London, lined with big houses and crooked trees, called Ulysses Way. Even before I moved in to No.33 I had the conviction I would meet either a Greek or an Irishman. I was not wrong. I met both: a Greek called Stavros, and Padraic Flynn. Also, there was – to come to first things first – Mrs C., the landlady.

I cannot bring myself to describe her in too much detail – she did not live on the premises but had a house somewhere in Finchley – because she looked ridiculous. An over-made- up middle-aged woman, with tinted spectacles, attired in a teenager's quasi-leather fashion gear. However, the crucial point about our landlady was not her appearance but her absenteeism, her not living on the premises.

Our landlady visited the house often, and not only on rent collection days, 'To see you've got no problems', frequently adding, 'I don't like you to have problems. I like you all to get on and be nice to each other.' Then, 'This is a nice house an' you all should keep it that way.' But if one does not actually dwell in a house – that is, sleep in it – one never really knows what goes on. Ghosts only walk at night. Consequently, Mrs C. did not appreciate what 'went on'. Instead, she had to rely on certain incompatibilities of experience – her own and that of any tenant who complained – to acquaint her with what life was really like at 33 Ulysses Way.

Ulysses Way itself was a noisy road. Partly because it was densely residential with innumerable restless cars stationed there; and, also, because it was used by motorists as a way of avoiding Cricklewood Broadway. Even so, one gets used to cars chasing boorishly up and down a street, or suddenly farting into life late at night. Cars constitute no interruption at all to conversation, or to the ceaseless train of thought, unless one happens to collide with another or brakes sensationally. Naturally, when the police arrive at 3 o'clock in the morning and arrest the Greek in room 2, who leaves loudly protesting in broken English and, doubtless, swearing in Greek, one doesn't get used to that sort of thing at all. Though when, the following day, on returning from one's work in the City, one sees the Greek laughing and gesticulating in the kitchen with Flynn, one does feel curious. More importantly, with the night raid, being just the first of many incidents large or small, one begins to build up rapidly that mental picture of what the collective rhythm of the place signifies. Through the variety of nocturnal sounds one begins to form an idea of the differing characters of one's neighbours.

Take Flynn again who, though his name rhymed with 'sin', was a bit of a saint, a nice man, but irritatingly illogical in his habits. He'd leave the communal cooker filthy, bang doors horrendously and only wash any of the available crockery when there was none left for him to eat off. This last forced everyone else, as crockery was shared, to wash his up for him, if they wished to have anything clean to eat off themselves. And it was the same with the kitchen waste bin which the dear man helped to fill but never emptied, with precious little thought for others. Still, he was very charming; and it gave one a sense of homeliness to emerge from one's room and find Padraic always lounging at the kitchen table ready with a smile or a nod or a torrent of polite enquiries about one's day. 'And how is the world with you today, my friend?'

Then there were 'the Fogs'. Why the Fogs? Because they had voices loud as a trio of foghorns! And though it was a solid old house, nonetheless, the unpreventable sound from below could be very disturbing. Fortunately, the Fogs departed for work early in the morning, leaving the house like overgrown kids setting out on an adventure. At least, they had alarm-clock value.

More distressing were 'the Tels': two telephone engineers who shared a double room on one side of mine. Most evenings they fell asleep with the T.V. on all night. Unable to sleep without it, they then snored heavily in (and out of) tune to an endless succession of programmes. Once a week, however, they varied their routine. At around two-thirty in the morning they would come in drunk. One of them was a Geordie; the other, the quieter of the two, a Midlander. I would be jerked out of my sleep by a series of crashings and stumblings up the short flight of stairs. Then I'd hear the Geordie bellow in an extremely rough voice, 'I swear...' (an ironical but accurate opening) 'I swear these fuggin' stairs will kill me wun of these fuggin' days!' Such being the me-awakening, gambit. Then, on one occasion having thus begun, the two men banged into their room, slammed the door shut, and promptly fell to fighting each other as well as the furniture. And when bodies are flying about in an adjacent room there is even greater scope for the aural imagination. It beats the creak of a floorboard any day, or I should say night. Murder seemed a certainty at the very least. But, in fact, the next morning – which I greeted bog-eyed and weary – I saw the two men set off to work as usual, still friends, and apparently unmarked!

Now, I'm not against lovers' tiffs. How can one be? They are natural. There are tensions in all creative pursuits. But when, at half-past three going on four in the morning, Rod and Linda (they were on the floor above) set about one another in ferocious style, that also was disturbing. Eventually, Rod – who was a shade over six foot in height in contrast to Linda's five foot four – fled naked save for a tee-shirt from their room and locked himself in the bathroom. While Linda, in tears and wailing like a Banshee from Battersea, was forced to spend the better (or should I say worse) part of an hour coaxing the frightened he-man out of that room.

Not all of one's neighbours, of course, were disturbing through abrupt appeals to one's sense of hearing. The very quiet Indian gentleman with the unpronounceable name – I called him Singh – his strategy was different. After telling me the unsurprising fact of the year, namely, 'I like Indian food!', he proceeded to spend most of the day in voluminous cooking. And he cooked such a pungent curry for breakfast that an early morning visit to the bathroom was like staggering and spluttering down a corridor filled with tear-gas.

Sometimes, interruptions to one's forlorn attempts at sleep could also come from outside the house. We never had an intruder, but we did have a hopeless drunk (Irish again) who had wandered up from Kilburn. He stationed himself directly outside no. 33 in the 'wee small hours' and vociferously demanded political change in Ireland. 'We want a united Ireland! We want a united Oireland! ... Come out and join me, you bastards, and together we can get the British troops out of Oireland! ... Oi knows yer all fuggin' awake – yer must be by now!' In this last he was certainly correct. After fifteen minutes of his drunken demagoguery, however, I had tiptoed downstairs to the pay phone in the hall and rung the police. Within two – yes two – minutes they'd arrived. I heard a voice outside in the street say politely, 'Now, sir, isn't it time you went home?' The drunk left like a lamb, and left me to count sheep to no avail ... as well as to marvel at the efficiency of the Metropolitan police in coming so quickly. In the morning I learned that four other people had sent for the police before me.

I was perhaps more than most of my fellow tenants inclined to keep to my room. Even so, it was impossible to avoid meeting Flynn who had set up a permanent talking shop in the kitchen. Which, in its way was no bad thing for, apart from the friendly atmosphere it generated, it meant that every tenant could know every other tenant's business without them actually meeting, simply by talking with Padraic.

In many people's eyes though – even such as might be exposed to his wonderful charm, his handsome demeanour and quickfire brogue – Padraic would be considered to have one important fault, the Irishman was constantly borrowing money. I cannot be sure if he borrowed from anyone other than myself. But borrow from me he certainly did. Fortunately, they were small sums – though over my two months stay they did mount up. From the moment he made his first borrowing, I said to myself, 'You can write this off, old son – he'll not repay it'. Also I recalled my late father's advice, 'Don't press a man too hard for repayment of a loan because he can't borrow again until he has paid you back'. The fine, unblinking eyes and film star smile gave the lie to that theory two days after the first borrowing, when Padraic asked me to lend him the Tube fare to somewhere in the West End. And so it went on, the odd fifty pence here for a loaf or a bus fare; ten pence there for a phone call; or now and then, enough for a pint at the pub. 'Could you be seein' your way to a small sum for ...?' was how he always opened the proceedings, in or out of banking hours!

'I have never liked the Irish,' confessed Mrs C. as she wrote out my receipt for the rent on only the second Saturday I was there.

Me, tentatively, 'Oh, I don't think one can generalize.'

She, 'You bleedin' can when you've had the sort of experiences I've had with the Irish!'

Someone had told her about Flynn's phone call in the middle of the night; an event that had probably woken everyone up. (It had come from a girl friend in America, he later told me.)

Then, when the call was over, he'd made himself a slap-up meal in the communal kitchen and sat whistling away to himself until dawn, before going to bed and sleeping until the early afternoon. None had shared his elation though, and someone had 'squealed' on him to our landlady.

I, too, had been so far irritated by the incident as to mention it to Flynn. He had been very embarrassed to hear it had disturbed my slumbers and promised profusely to try and ensure it never happened again. As far as I am aware, it never did. But at the time I was listening to Mrs C.'s complaints about the Irishman, I couldn't be sure it wouldn't recur. It was my somewhat vague defence of Flynn's nocturnal conduct, and my gushing, 'Oh, Mrs C., he's such a nice fellow', that had led to my landlady's outburst. Until, at length, I found myself waiting to hear more of her 'sort of experiences' with the Irish.

She confessed, 'I had one here once who knifed his wife and then terrorized all the other tenants ... Now that ain't no behaviour for a decent place, is it?'

Well, of course, I could see immediately why she was so touchy about the Irish. Still, I persisted that Flynn was a decent fellow, a bit illogical and careless, but very decent.

Decency! It was from that moment onwards, every single time I conversed with Mrs C. up came the subject of decency. 'It is a decent house I like to keep here. Decency is so important, know what I mean?'

But what had she really got against Flynn? Apart from her bad memory of a former murderous Irish tenant, it seemed all she could hold against Padraic were a few minor complaints from him about lack of soap and toilet paper about the place. Small irritations which I had overcome by purchasing such necessaries and keeping them in my room.

Doubtless a solution practiced by the rest of the tenants, save the skint Irishman. But none of this seemed to justify why Mrs C. had 'so taken against me', as Padraic put it, being well aware of the situation. For, certainly by the standard of behaviour set, night after night, by the Tels, the Fogs, and the young lovers, Flynn was a paradigm of decency.

As the weeks rolled on and I became fully aware of Mrs C.'s attitude, I saw the dichotomy between her view of the rest of the tenants, and what she thought of Flynn. Speaking of 'the quiet young gentlemen in rooms one and three, and that lovely young couple in the studio upstairs', it was obvious she had a completely wrong notion as to how things really were at the house. She genuinely thought we were all living harmoniously together with 'that Flynn the only fly in the ointment'.

It did not take me long to realize that all of us – myself included – were really responsible for her misjudgement of the young Irishman. For no one had complained to her of the misbehaviour of any of the other tenants. No one, however, not me, nor Singh (who only beamed at everyone and everything), nor Flynn had uttered a peep to Mrs C. about the far more serious and downright inconsiderate behaviour of the Tels; or of the constant yawping and bellowing of the Fogs; nor told of the pseudo-marital post-coition ding-dongs of Rod and Linda. And, for some reason, the brief arrest of Stavros had not reached our landlady's ears either. Consequently, Mrs C. had been allowed to languish in her misconception of the true state of affairs.

One night the Tels arrived back as per drunken usual and as per drunken late. They were bellowing and arguing. The Tel-in-Chief, the Geordie, tripped and fell on the stairs hurting some part of his anatomy (I doubt it was his head). This led once more to an immoderate kicking of the inanimate stairs to which he still attributed human fornicatory proclivities. Then, out of the midst of this welter of obscenities, emerged a complaint indirectly against our absentee landlady. Bawled he, 'There's nivver any bleedin' lights workin' in this place, man!' An observation half-true at least, for the full complement of light bulbs in the place was never complete. To which the other, equally inebriated Tel, retorted philosophically, 'Yer only gets wot yer pays for!'

This struck me as an especially interesting remark despite its triteness. For the truth was that at 33 Ulysses Way you didn't get what you paid for. Mrs C. overcharged for her rooms – hence the reason why one or two were often empty for weeks on end. Although the tenants paid above the market rate, they certainly didn't get proportionately superior accommodation. Which told me another inescapable truth about our landlady. Not only was she absentee, she was avaricious as well. Despite this, however, I still did not find it easy to make any equation between Mrs C.'s greed and obsession with decency, and her firm belief that it was only Flynn who threatened the house's stability.

One evening, towards the end of my stay in Ulysses Way, I was walking home from the Tube station. It was a bright, cool time of the day; the sun having not quite shot its bolt, and Spring was murmuring and rustling in all the scant gardens thereabouts. I saw a figure approaching in my direction fantastically weighed down with carrier bags, a shoulder sack (no other description for it), and two huge suitcases. As the distance between us shrank, I recognized Flynn. We met and halted face to face.

'Good God!' I exclaimed, 'where are you taking all that stuff?'

Padraic smiled beautifully, but ruefully. 'Out on the streets tis I am,' he replied.

I frowned. 'What do you mean? You've left our happy homestead?'

'Not, surely, by my own will. But herself has given me my marching orders, so she has.'

'But why ... you are the life and soul of that place?'

'Ah, that is as may be, an' all thanks to you for saying it. If I could think of a line from my master Rummy, I'd deliver it as a blessing on you! But just now t'is only black curses that fill me mind.' He said this with feeling.

'Yes ... but why has the old harridan slung you out?'

'Tis the rent, you see? I was some days behind.'

I knew that phrase, 'some days', as belonging firmly to what I call 'subjective mathematics'; and I just had to query it.

'And how many, Padraic, is 'some days'?' I demanded suspiciously.

'Only three weeks, I swear to God!' he cried, 'An' that only because me cheque hasn't arrived.' His voice grew more 'Irish' the more excited he became. 'Tree weeks!' he repeated. I knew he spoke the truth. For just three weeks' arrears our absentee landlady had thrown him out. Had made this delightful young man homeless. For a few pieces of silver ... I didn't know what to say.

98

Moved, I asked, '

'Where will you ...?' Then in a blaze of anger-pity took out my wallet and extracting all the notes thrust them in his top pocket, after which I abruptly hurried on. He called out something after me but I didn't stop.

As for me, I managed to survive my remaining time in Ulysses Way. And continued to 'keep myself to myself' as much as possible before going back to my home in Devon.

15.
REMEMBERING KEN SMITH

A small ferry, a blue and white cork on water, took their fancy: Ken Smith and his wife, the American poet Judi Benson. Not a likely place for the once dubbed 'hard man of British poetry', the tory-blue waters of Torbay. But they loved it, especially their little trips on *The Shepherd Lass*, the underdog ferry of a bay dominated by the grander, sleeker *Western Lady*. Still, Ken was always very English in his sympathy for society's less-than-fortunates; and even when I asked him why he didn't take the bigger ferry, better stabilized and 'with a bar on it', he gave a slight negative headshake, said, 'Nope. The little 'un's just fine.' His voice was still North Yorkshire – brackish stream, whiskey-coloured over hard rocks – but with some American clipping round the edges. The Middle English of Langland had, somewhere, met the make-it-new of Pound, O'Hara and Bly. A wonderful voice that, like Dylan Thomas's, recorded well but was natural, guttural, non-declamatory.

Drawn to Ken through his poetry, I was pleased he came to Torbay for its first Poetry Festival. On one previous occasion Patricia and I had hosted a reading for him – or rather Patricia had and I was there – and that had been at Westfield College, Hampstead in about 1990. After the reading he and Judi stayed in our campus room into the small hours eating and drinking with us. So late, in fact, that one presumed they must have caught a cab back to East Ham. (But when I asked them about this later, they insisted that they'd caught the last local train from West Hampstead – at 1.30am?). 'They didn't want to go, did they?' Patricia had observed. It was true. They were warm people in a friendless world, and I see Ken now, wine glass in hand, seated under the wonderful poster Bloodaxe Books had done for him when they were trying to hype him as the Lone Ranger from Rudston. That poster now adorns a corner of our house in Brixham; it has his signature on the chin, where he took most of life.

In the visitors' book at 6 The Mount, he said of the Torbay Festival, 'Long may she sail the bay. The captain is sober and the ship sails at midnight'. That the captain of the Festival Ship was sober, Ken found rather intimidating. I asked him several times to have a drink and, remarkably, he refused – and this was the day *before* his 'event'. 'I've gotta stay sober for the sergeant major', he muttered gloomily, and went off and sat on the steps of the Princess Theatre, Torquay: a Rodin figure in May sunlight that came blindingly off a crisp, brisk sea. Variously, the 'captain' or 'sergeant major' was, of course, Patricia, the Festival organizer. Soon after, someone said to me, 'Ken's sat on the steps of the theatre with his head in his hands – what's the matter with him?' I answered, 'The bar's clo.... he's, er, rehearsing for his reading tonight.' An answer which satisfied no-one.

The Livermead House Hotel – all red sandstone and flowers – gave us a charming dining room, which opened onto a terrace with bay views, for the Festival supper. It is a two-story hotel, Devon-farmhouse-style, and the Victorian poet-novelist Charles Kingsley wrote part of *The Water Babies* there. In the elegant room with marble fireplace, piano and ornate mirrors, we had a gracious meal. Then, over coffee, Ken was to read. It fell to me to introduce him and I spoke not long but used a phrase that had occurred to me, describing him – or his poetry really – as 'a romantic-realist'. This was not a phrase, I think, that those critics of his work, always bent on emphasizing its hard edge and contemporary relevance, would have ever used. They would quote lines like:

They never complain
to whom nothing is promised

or

here among the rich invisibles
copyholders of Budleigh Salterton

the stoical and the bitterly humorous. Whereas, for me, the truer Ken Smith was the poet who captures, evokes the still sad music of humanity and of Nature: and at that he was a consummate artist:

This was my first love
the numerous wind through grass.

But a deep regret entered him, even in that childhood-time, and it came about because his father, a poor agricultural labourer in North Yorkshire, was forced to abandon the struggle against the elements and become a shopkeeper:

Silence is gone from their lives, the city
has taken that poised energy ...
seasons pass them without touching.
They will not feel the winter when it comes.

Nevertheless, to my surprise, after that reading, Ken said he thought 'romantic-realist' was 'pretty accurate as these things go.'

As time went by, Ken grew into a rootless being, a wanderer, an outsider (however much though, like Peter Russell and other marginalized poets, he may have craved fame's acceptance) and was always to stay that way. He was a good man at heart (where it counts) but there was a wire run through it and he became restless. Yes, he found 'base' in relationship – especially with the remarkable Judi, and their place in London's East End. But the call of distant places kept getting to him, so he would take off now and then, whether running like his famous fox all around London's Tube system, which replicates the chthonic dismal, hellish underground; or to far flung places like Columbia, or the Cuba that killed him in the end.

But did he have any kind of faith or was he always a searcher? I think for a long time he was a socialist utopian – maybe he remained so – but the sudden collapse of Eastern Europe's outposts of that utopia, followed by the fall of communism's soviet mecca, compelled him to re-examine his 'belief'. He had to go to Eastern Europe, he had to be there when the tide of change was washing away the Berlin Wall (and wrote a book about that cataclysmic event). Already a ghost-haunted man, relatively late in life he went to meet fresh ghosts to, perhaps, provide him with some clues as to why the whole world was now but one dystopia. He went to East Germany, Poland, Hungary etc. and (I believe) his last slim volume – published appropriately in Hungary – is the finest of siftings of this late experience, this search. Two things stand out in that volume, the extraordinary historical sequence on the final campaign of Islam in Eastern Europe, that of Suliman the Magnificent. Ken called the poem 'The Shadow of God' and I'd first read it with surprise in a Welsh magazine, thinking it was 'not Ken's sort of thing'. But I realize now he had gone back to historical basics to try and understand why Eastern Europe had failed to sustain the socialist ideal. This volume, copies of which I waved at the Festival's dinner guests, was called *Wire Through the Heart*, and one of the poems has these lines:

> And who
> would have thought in all the
> siftings of the stars I'd be here,
> an old man with his tobacco?
> Surely we are all heaven's dust. All's well.

Sentiments truly remarkable for the hard, gloomy, working-class cowboy poet as we were all supposed to see him? A poem, ending that Browningesque way, written to his love:

> from the collapsing country
> across the shifting borders.

I cannot recall whether Ken actually read that poem, called 'Heaven's Dust', at the Festival supper, but I do recall him launching forth into some of his new translations from *Piers Plowman*. A remarkable experience for the two dozen or so dinner guests to be exposed to the real thew and sinew of Middle-English brilliantly modernized. A kind of reality to which culturally-deprived Torbay was unused! Yet everyone knew that evening they were encountering a real poet who followed Sir Philip Sydney's advice to the letter: always writing (and translating) from the heart, wire or no wire.

After it was over, there was an exquisitely relaxing time in which I said to Ken, 'You'll have a drink now?' He nodded and partook of several very large vodkas and orange, before he was driven, sleepy and happy, to The Smuggler's Haunt Hotel in Brixham. Where an interrupted night's sleep awaited him because of Torbay's curse of herring gulls. As Judi wrote in a poem called 'Sleepless in Brixham':

> There's no baby abandoned
> on the window sill,
> just gulls ...
> words drift you through
> the sleepless room
> always on the edge of gull.

And what words were they? Words providing a sense of the many impressions of the Festival thus:

Just William with his rain-fall stories
down on all 4's, Les on his banjo
that pickled onion song again,
the sgt. major checking to see
everyone has their orders.
If only she'd give one
to the wind, the bamboo, the gulls.

I'd told a story about a fall I'd had in the rain; Les Jones, the Bard of Babbacombe, played his song about 'the biggest pickled onion in the world' to the accompaniment of his ukulele at Ken's event; and the sergeant major was ... but that's already been explained.

One of Ken Smith's hobbies was the making of masks. Danielle Hope wrote a poem about this. It has the lines:

... the mask-maker's hands
smooth the chin
to match the curve of the heart.

Ken was a very private person but one thrust by poetry into the limelight, the public arena. To protect his privacy he made masks and they were a projection of his many psychological masks. I have many memories of him. Like the time in the bar at Cambridge University Students' Union we spent with him and Eddie Linden, and Eddie was on good form, which in anyone else's vocabulary would be, well, a wonderful 'form' of maybe patience-testing, bar-emptying eccentricity. Even so, Ken wrote 'The Ballad of Eddie Linden', and he didn't do that for anyone else. And Ken came to the somewhat eccentric launch of my *Collected Longer Poems* – with its magnificent buffet paid for by a total stranger, a Russian – at the old Turret Bookshop. Afterwards, the event moved on to an Italian restaurant, courtesy of that much missed patron of poets, the bookseller Bernard Stone. At that meal, Ken showed a clowning side to his otherwise serious nature – a sort of chicken-lickin' cowboy humour. It was at events like these which enabled me to get to know Ken. But I suppose only Judi really knew him well. Though we all knew he was a true poet who did not hide his real humanity from his friends.

More varied still than his masks, real or metaphorical, were his poems; or, rather, his range of subject matter. Jon Glover, in a fine obituary for Ken, acclaimed him a great poet. It is, of course, far too early to prejudge posterity's view. But one of the essential preconditions of greatness in a poet, is range and variety of work; another is humility; and a third is loyalty to the truth. At different times, at parties, literary events, over dinner or at the First Torbay Poetry Festival, Ken allowed me brief glimpses of all those three things. They testify to the possibility of a favourable judgment from posterity at the very least, and I am content with that.

16.
OUR LIFE IS NOT OUR OWN

In the mid-Nineties I received a letter from the doctor's surgery at which I was registered, apparently. Expressed in faintly accusatory tones, it informed me that I had not 'visited the Practice for three years'. In fact, I had never visited the Practice in the quarter of a century I had lived with my family in Brixham – at least, not on my own account. However, faced with this medical equivalent of a police summons, Patricia suggested I availed myself of it and went for a health check-up. This I duly did, and it led to my having an annual overhaul at the holy-sounding St. Luke's Surgery in Brixham's New Road.

At one of these, carried out by a female doctor of attractive demeanour, I received the unwelcome information, health-wise, that while my blood-pressure and other things were extraordinarily good for a 'man of my age', my liver was receiving too much alcoholic aggro.

'Binge drinking is inadvisable at any age, Mr. Oxley, so I strongly advise you to reduce your intake – then come back and see me in three months.' Mixed health news indeed – all of which, later, I imparted to Patricia. As to her reaction, it was simply to utter the one word, 'Well?' which I knew really meant, 'What are you going to do about it then?'

I told her, nobly and logically, there was little point in voluntarily, or involuntarily in my case, seeking medical advice if, having received it, one was not prepared to follow it. So that is what I resolved upon doing, namely, cutting down on my boozing.

It was not long before I encountered the first difficulty, and one designed especially for social drinkers such as myself. Shortly after my medical showdown, Patricia and I were staying at our friend Danielle's house situated on the banks of the Regent's Canal in London. Danielle is quite often out at work when we turn up; but she always leaves a plentiful supply of red wine for me to attack. But when, after two days, she noticed I had not opened a single bottle, she demanded to know why. Had I 'taken the pledge?' Was I 'unwell, or what'? Thinking on my feet I told her I was resolved 'to enter the London Marathon' the following year. Consequently, I felt that I needed, as a first step towards getting fit, to cut down on my drinking. For a man of my age – and one who never even runs for a bus – it seemed a surprising revelation.

What is more, to Danielle – herself a doctor too – it appeared, to say the least, a resolution of folly.

'Why would you be doing it ... really ?' she asked.

''Er, to raise money for the Torbay Poetry Festival.'

'How will running a marathon achieve that?'

'I will try to get sponsors who will sponsor me so much per mile – but only to be paid if I finish the race.'

So it was, that weekend – one of parties and poetry readings – it became known why I was struggling to control my customary imbibing of alcohol. In fact, I ended the weekend with four sponsors: there was Patricia at £1 a mile; a publisher friend at a similar sum; plus my ever-generous friend David Beugger. who promised 1p per mile (once upon a time very philanthropic, with age David had become parsimonious); and an artist friend who said she would sponsor me for so much per mile but forgot to sign my list of would-be sponsors.

Returning to Brixham after the handful of days away 'up in the Smoke', I realized I was stuck now with a host of public explanations (ie. for my small public) as to why I wished to imitate Pheidippides' ancient feat of running from Marathon to Athens. So, to begin with, I tried to continue to 'pace' my drinking, beginning by cutting out spirits entirely: a sort of 'shorts cut' as I thought of it. Though I had, as yet, to run a single yard. But I felt that running practice could come later when I had out-paced, mentally-speaking, the demon drink. In my mind, there was an errant poet galloping, half out of breath, along an endless Dantean circle pursued by a devil called Breweezijug.

But things change, frequently, at The Mount. If it is not total strangers turning up like the sudden arrival of some Polish poets, the youngest among whom had limited English and was virtually stone-deaf, then it is receiving unexpected invitations. Some of which arouse one's interest, if only because one has not the least idea why one should have been sent such. Like, for example, the invitation that awaited me on our return from London. It was from the Army, and went thus: 'Brigadier So and So, requests the pleasure of your company at the Grand Hotel, Torquay etc. etc.' As the occasion included, first, a drinks' reception, then a presentation about the work of the modern army, finishing with 'a finger buffet' and more drinks, the occasion appealed, despite my training regimen.

The Army? Appealing to a poet? Whatever next? But, let me explain. I had always had three ambitions in life. My first ambition was to be a poet or, rather, to write some good poems. My second had always been to be an actor. In small measure my Shakespearean 'bit' parts had fulfilled that ambition. But third on my life careers' wish list had been the desire to be a general in the Army. Because of ill-health as a child I never even qualified for National Service. Unlike my pal Tony who tells how, almost single-handedly, he prevented the Communist hordes from over-running Malaya; or unlike a poet acquaintance of mine who 'horizontally jogged' his way through the same campaign in native girls' huts and brothels around Singapore. But that, in my understanding at least, was why the invitation from the Army appealed. As I was about to find out, however, the 'appeal' of the Army has another meaning.

The newly-refurbished Grand Hotel, Torquay, is a very swell place. Patricia accompanied me on the appropriate evening, and we met up with our friend Danny Pyle who runs the Torquay Writers Group. As an ex-serviceman, inviting Danny made more sense than inviting me. He was accompanied by two friends, female members of his writers' group.

Despite my recent resolve to attain athletic fitness, I was among the first to find themselves in the drinks' reception. At that point, the majority of persons present were soldiers kitted out in camouflage fatigues, save for a couple of the highest ranked officers who were in khaki uniforms with red epaulettes. Scarcely had I obtained my glass of wine at the door and entered the room, before I was accosted by a handsome young man with a faint Northern Irish accent whom, it turned out, was a major. He engaged me in conversation, explaining that he and his colleagues were there to help enlighten the guests about the work of the modern British army and to answer any questions about it. Then his eye fell on the plastic identity badge affixed to my shirt front. It read '*William Oxley: Poet*'. Those present, according to the letter from the Army, were supposed to be Torbay's civic dignitaries and 'opinion-formers'. Unaware, I think, of the irony in his question, the major asked, 'A Poet? Why...er...are you here?' As my response was unhelpful, namely, 'I can't say', he quickly recovered himself by way of tactical withdrawal: 'Afraid I don't go in for flowery writing ...' This only compounded his difficulties but, if the pun may be forgiven, he soldiered on, 'I only have use in my profession for direct, simple and plain speech – economical ...' At that point, Patricia, who had joined us, informed him that, in fact, poetry was capable of a brevity impossible in prose, but we both could see that he did not grasp that point at all. However, he instinctively knew he had got himself into a situation out of which he must fight his way. So he said in a kind of cool desperation,

'What inspires you to write poetry?'

'Everything and nothing.' said I.

'Have you had any inspiration this evening?' He blithely went on.

'Not so far.'

'Might you?'

'Can't say'.

Fortunately, at this junction we were interrupted. It was time for us all to take our seats in the lecture hall (the hotel's ballroom) for the Army's Presentation of 'All we do for you, the taxpayers'. It proved mostly interesting – if not exactly riveting – and covered everything from the current war situation in Afghanistan, to things like the assistance the army had rendered locally in neighbouring Cornwall at Boscastle during the previous year's flood disaster which had struck that town.

But enough of purely military matters (an attitude which may provide a clue to my unfulfilled ambition to be another Wellington or Montgomery?). Scarcely had I settled in to eating – or 'getting it down my neck' to use squaddies' language – some food and drink at the so-called 'finger-buffet', than the Major approached me again. As, in fact, he would continue to do until we had finally left the hotel for home. It was obvious that he had never met a poet and, despite his disavowals of interest in poetic language, he was fascinated. Obviously, in his experience I was – though a mere human like himself – some sort of exotic species. Had I had any inspiration yet? Did I anticipate writing any poems out of the event later?

Then, joined by others, he continued his interrogation of me. One question I do particularly recall: What was it actually inspired me to write? The question I had already answered, or so I thought. 'Have you not heard of art through suffering?' He looked at me startled. 'Poets ...' I added, 'are inspired by suffering ... suffering or drink ...

sometimes both.' He and the others laughed. 'You should be in the army,' he said to more laughter

The final time the Major appeared at my side that evening he informed me that, 'After this Presentation we are all being drafted next month to Afghanistan.' I knew of course that a contingent of 8,000 troops were being sent to assist the American forces fighting the Taliban guerrillas on the remote border between Afghanistan and Pakistan – it had been in all the newspapers. Indeed, when the Taliban had destroyed the gigantic statues of the Buddhas of Bamyan, I had written a poem entitled 'Bang, Bang, Taliban': a poem which a student at the University of Salzburg had analyzed in great detail.

What I was not prepared for however was what the Major said next. 'Look,' he went on, 'this poetry thing. Would you like to come to Afghanistan as poet-in-residence with the Army? You'd get plenty to inspire you there.'

I reflected for a moment. Thinking of how inspiring I had found my visit to Nepal at the other end of the Himalayas. 'Yes, I'd like to go. I don't know what the wife will think about it of course ... but write me a letter of proposal.'

I did not hear from the Army again. But it quite threw into confusion my plan to enter the London Marathon. After all, one could not train simultaneously for two such different ventures. So, while continuing to view with a wary eye my AA demons' encroaching, I did little but watch each day for the arrival of the postman and continued to write poems as and when I was moved to do so. I remained intrigued though by the thought of what it would have been like to be a poet-in-residence with an army regiment? And a year or two later I saw a newspaper report that a much younger poet than myself had received just such an offer from the Military. But whether the offer was taken up I have not subsequently heard. Maybe he opted to run the London Marathon instead?

17.
OSTRACISM BY PROXY

This is what happened. In the late Eighties my wife wished to obtain a university place to study for a mature student's degree. She was well-qualified to take such a place, being in possession of all requisite paper qualifications: indeed she was almost over-qualified, one might say. For, not only did she have all the usual school certificates in the best grades but, as she desired to do a degree in English literature, she could demonstrate a long and wide experience of prose and poetry through her continued editorial commitment to running her own literary journal, *Acumen*. Additionally, she had had a scientific training, having been employed for some years in the field of chemistry; and had successfully raised two daughters – with a modest degree of assistance from her husband. In short, there was no way Patricia was not a gift to any university. Indeed, one eminent fellow editor thought she was already a practicing academic and 'not a mere student'.

After some deliberation, she opted to try for a place at one of the London universities – preferably as close as possible to the centre of the metropolis. It was where she and I wished to be if we were to spend three years in London – partly to be near friends, bookshops and the like. And the three university colleges which came into the frame were King's College in the Strand, Queen Mary & Westfield in Hampstead and Mile End, and University College in Gower Street. Any one of these was suitably situated for our purposes. And having gone through the customary universities' application procedures, Patricia was offered interviews at all three. This is how those interviews went.

At the first, there were two interviewers – both male – whose 'technique' it seemed was that of presenting themselves as a Professor Nasty and a Professor Nice – standard third-degree method. The chief interviewer was a small Scotsman behind a big desk, silver-haired, and by name of Karl Miller. Most persons in those days of a literary bent had heard of Miller: author of many books and articles and, amongst other things he was an early editor of *The London Review of Books* and a man who had occupied a number of other important literary posts. A figure of significance in that amorphous cultural and political grouping which had come to be very dominant in London affairs, bookish and otherwise, which another Scot, the journalist Andrew Neil, described as 'the Tartan Raj'. Karl Miller had also been closely associated with Ian Hamilton's little magazine *The Review*: one of the three or four most significant such periodicals of the Sixties and Seventies.

The first question that was put to Patricia was a demand to know why she wished to come to the capital at all, seeing it was – in Miller's view – a place of great risk to anyone, but especially women, from muggers and rapists and other criminal elements. Patricia declined to be drawn on this point, or to retort with the query that if London was so dangerous a place why was the diminutive professor himself still there? Actually, he may not have been quite so small as his big desk made him appear seated – but like any Scot with a chip on his shoulder he was forced to stoop closer to the ground.

'Are you related to William Oxley?'

'Yes.'

'The same William Oxley who edited *Littack* in the 1970's?'

'Yes.'

An even more anxious query followed, 'If you were to come to London would you bring your, er, husband with you?'

'Yes,' she answered again.

Karl Miller fell silent, leaving the nameless but nice professor to try and ask more relevant interview questions such as "What are you reading at the moment?"

'Kathleen Raine.'

This produced another outburst from Professor Nasty, directed against certain poets such as the mystically-inclined and still living Kathleen Raine, or the long-dead Samuel Taylor Coleridge who were regarded as 'unsound'. Her interest in such unsound writers, plus a husband who was very much an Unapproved Poet, meant that she was also unlikely to prove academically sound. Then Miller, much to the surprise of Professor Nice, began inveighing against mature students in general, saying 'They never do well!'

'But how about...?' interrupted his colleague, naming a particular mature student then on the course.

Miller glared at him, 'An exception. Most mature students don't do well at all!' He added again for good measure what had become almost a mantra throughout the interview, 'And you won't like London!'

Unsurprisingly, Patricia was not offered a place at UCL

In those days it was our practice to take the daily National Express bus to London and, if timing went well, we could make it to an interview up in the Smoke and get back to Brixham in the same day. Which is what we did the day she went for her second interview which was at King's College in the Strand. I, of course, did not attend the interviews but spent the time in book shops and bars. And she and I would meet up again somewhere afterwards – usually at Victoria coach station.

I shall never forget Patricia striding somewhat sternly towards me at the coach station, nor her first question to me,

'Do you know a man called...?' and she named him.

'Can't say I do. Should I?'

Still talking volubly, Patricia led the way onto the double-decker coach, 'Well, he knows all about you. What's more he has all the issues of *Littack* – even says he was a subscriber...So I thought you might know him?'

'Nope,' I said as we seated ourselves, adding, 'How did the interview go then?'

'Difficult to say, but I'm fairly sure it will be another turn down.'

'What? Because of *Littack* again?' I felt angry.

'Maybe that...and other things.'

'What other things?'

'Well, X and his colleague – a woman professor this time who clearly was his superior – took great interest in the fact that I also edited a poetry magazine. They both snatched at the same time at the copy of *Acumen* I had brought with me and both perused it in turn, completely ignoring me for several minutes. Then X asked if I would continue to run the magazine if I got a place at university. I said I would. To which he said in some surprise, as I was clearly already at "the sharp end" of contemporary poetry, what could they possibly teach me? "Plenty," I told him, "about other periods than the present"'

'It was then he asked if I was related to you, showing his knowledge of *Littack*. But I didn't go through the rigmarole this time. I told him straight out that, Yes, you were my husband and, yes, if I moved to London you would be coming with me.' She paused, then added thoughtfully, 'You know, for someone whose job it is to teach students something of the finer points of English literature from its beginnings down to today, he seemed profoundly unconvinced that anyone could actually be keen to take the course. But, at least, neither he, nor his colleague, held mature students in the contempt that Professor Nasty (aka the late Karl Miller) did.'

Despite, however, returning to Devon that day in a slightly more optimistic frame of mind, Patricia was not offered a place at King's College either.

Third time is often said to be lucky, and so it proved. Our visit to Queen Mary & Westfield College in Kiderpore Gardens, London NW3 was a success. And no one mentioned me or *Littack* in what Patricia reported was an enjoyable interview. Though there was some resistance to Patricia's ideas – Kathleen Raine and Coleridge were still thought 'unsound' – she had three good years at that college, coming away with a first class honours' degree.

A small, ironical twist occurred to this tale of what I have termed ostracism by proxy, one evening when we both attended a literary function at King's College in the Strand. The occasion was the first 'Adam Lecture' funded by a bequest from the distinguished magazine *Adam International Review,* then coming to the end of its life. *Adam* was edited by a highly-eccentric Central European called Miron Grindea who had published a long poem of mine.

After the lecture – given by my old friend Anthony Rudolf from *Littack* days – there was a drinks' reception. At this reception I encountered Eric Mottram who was the then senior professor of the English Literature Department at King's. In the course of our talk, he asked me – wait for it! – was I 'married to Patricia Oxley?', and if I was, was she present? I replied in the double affirmative, and Mottram promptly asked to meet her. I had already told him that she had just 'graduated with a First' from QMW.

Having introduced them, I left them together. Very briefly Patricia tells of the conversation that then ensued. If brevity is the soul of wit according to Shakespeare, it can also be sometimes the soul of revenge.

Asked Mottram, 'Why did you not come to King's to do your degree?'

'Because you lot turned me down.' She answered simply.

18.
LIVING GHOSTS or THE ART OF OBITUARY

Strange things happen in the poetry world. I remember Kathleen Raine telling me about Robin Skelton, a well-known academic poet of some years ago; she remarked casually one day, 'Robin has gone over to the witches'. Having emigrated from Manchester to Victoria in British Columbia, he had gone through a series of transformations from practising poet, to editor of *The Malahat Review* at the University of Victoria, to 'speaking for the witches' at one of Kathleen's conferences held at Dartington Hall in Devon, to, finally, a scholar bent on writing a book on every verse form in the world. This last enterprise he told Patricia and me of in person, but it was a project overtaken – not surprisingly given its impossible magnitude by Robin's death. The point of my writing of this is to suggest that poetry seems somehow to be haunted not only by ghosts of the dead, but by living ones too. Or so it seems when a poet one once knew, but who vanished from the scene, suddenly reappears many years later.

In the early Seventies when I was editing my combative journal *Littack,* I became involved with a number of poets – two in particular. One was the exiled Peter Russell, a poet originally from the Bristol area, and something of a polymath. The other poet of relevance here was Richard Burns, an academic from Cambridge.

Russell was a romantic bohemian and arguably the last real disciple of Ezra Pound, having been an intimate of the American modernist in the latter's old age. As I wrote at the time, 'Russell is the multilingual poet Pound only dreamed of becoming'. Though English by birth, Russell (as was then fashionable to do) claimed Celtic ancestry. He was a wayward, difficult character, visionary, and though no academic often seemed to half-hanker after becoming one: on his stationery when he lived in Italy he always styled himself 'Professore'. At first sight, the Cambridge-educated Richard Burns did not seem the sort of person who would be attracted to Peter Russell. But he was. Russell became for Burns a great mentor; and I believe that Burns and his first wife spent some time living in Venice to be near Russell, who was resident in that city for many years.

As part of my poetic mythmaking, along with publishing the

magazine *Littack*, I also endeavoured to start a movement in poetics which I named 'vitalism'. I even published two manifestoes intended as the theoretical programme of the movement. Of course, it came to very little. It didn't set the Thames on fire. But I was young and optimistic. Russell was very enthusiastic about it and was responsible for persuading Burns to contribute a lengthy written response to the manifestoes to be published in the magazine. In fact, four such responses were eventually forthcoming: Russell's own, Burns's, Brian Keeble and a third by Anthony Johnson, who became soon after the Professor of English at the University of Pisa. Burns, I have to say, took much more coaxing to obtain his contribution than with the others. When it appeared it was something of a surrealistic farrago, but I published it.

Fairly soon after the publication of his piece in *Littack,* Burns distanced himself from the magazine, from vitalism, and from me. It was never entirely clear to me why. Also, though he was a well-published poet, enjoying the privilege of books from a well-thought-of press, after a while – like Robin Skelton's 'going over to the witches' – Richard Burns faded from the poetry scene. Abruptly as he had come into my life, he left it: and, it seemed, the business of poetry as well. Through Elaine Feinstein, Peter Russell and Anthony Rudolf – who were always more closely associated with Burns than I was – I received the occasional snippet of gossip about him, but never anything sufficient to enable me to get a picture of his subsequent career. So I forgot Richard Burns.

In October 2000 I visited the Kingdom of Nepal. It proved one of the most moving and exciting experiences of my life. A day or two after returning home, I received a telephone call. The voice at the other end was wheezily warm, not quite oily. It said, 'William. Hi, this is Richard…Richard Burns. How are you?' You'd have thought we'd only parted the day before, not a quarter of a century ago!

My response was formal, cool, non-committal. I could feel myself becoming tense at this voice from the past – this living ghost. I had no wish to resume the relationship after so long. I felt like I guess we will all feel at the Day of Judgement when all our pasts catch up with us, and everyone who has known us will come into God's witness box to testify for us or, more likely, against us.

The formalities over, Burns went on, 'Have you heard about Peter Russell and the place they've moved him to in Tuscany?'

By then Peter, old and virtually blind, clearly a dying man, had been transferred by the local authorities to a nursing home. The ancient, crumbling watermill where he had lived for many years at a peppercorn rental due to some Tuscan aristocrat, was no longer somewhere he could go on living among damp, rats and his many books. His removal by officialdom had taken place not long before. I knew all about it through Kathleen Raine, as well as from Glyn Pursglove my Swansea friend who was Russell's literary executor and frequently visited the old poet. So, yes, I was informed about Russell's predicament, and about the fantastic generosity of the local mayor of Castel Franco who, despite having suffered many insults at the hands of 'the great poet', still felt it his duty to have Russell cared for. Italian magnaminity is largely reserved for artists, poets and opera singers.

'We should do something to help Peter, as his friends…' began Richard, 'He has no money and is living off the charity of the local mayor. I think we should try to get some funding from the Royal Literary Fund. I've already got the necessary forms. But I need his friends to write testimonials – I've already asked Kathleen Raine and William Cookson and they've agreed. Will you and Patricia do the same?'

I agreed, but pointed out that Russell had been the recipient already of moneys from the Royal Literary Fund – an organization that helps writers in straightened circumstances.

'Yes, but that was more than three years ago. The rules allow us to apply again now. But I can't do the forms without answering some questions about Peter's financial situation. Do you know what income he has, if any?'

'I think he receives a civil list pension from the Crown; and he may have a pension from the Italian authorities. But I don't know how much in either case. But why don't you get in touch with Glyn Pursglove. I happen to know he's going out to see Russell this coming week.'

'Glyn who? Who's he?'

'Glyn Pursglove…he's Peter Russell's literary executor. And an academic like yourself.'

This piece of information Richard was pleased to have. I explained that Glyn was also Patricia's reviews' editor for her magazine. For the purpose of Richard's project this piece of information was crucial. And, in the following week, he and Glyn met up at Stanstead Airport in

Essex, or at Cambridge, and Glyn became the essential informational conduit enabling the RLF application to be made to help one more impecunious writer survive a bit longer than otherwise might have been the case.

The following January, but a mere two months later, Patricia and I received a badly scrawled, round robin but deeply touching letter from Peter Russell expressing heartfelt thanks to his friends for securing the handsome sum of £21,000 to help pay for his care in the nursing home in Castel Franco, Provincia Arezzo. I wrote straight back saying that, in truth, the real credit should go to Burns who was the prime mover in the affair. At the same time, I contacted Richard to congratulate him on the success of *his* project. My estimate of him had risen a great deal; and I quite forgave him the difficulties which, as I imagined, he had caused me in the past.

About a year later, I encountered Richard at the party at Christies for the relaunched *London Magazine*. Following the death of its editor Alan Ross, who had edited the magazine for many years, it had a new owner; plus a new editor in the person of my old friend Sebastian Barker. I discovered, too, that Richard had started to publish poetry again.

A further year on from that literary gathering, Peter Russell died; and Richard Burns again rang me up. This is what he proposed, 'I think we should get together a little team to do obituaries of Peter in the newspapers. I am going to do The Indie…' (by which I deduced he meant *The Independent*) 'Which one would you like to do?' Before I could answer he added, 'I've been on the phone to Glyn, and he's willing to do the one for The Guardian. So it's The Telegraph or The Times for you.'

'Er, well, I'll do The Times then.'

'Are you sure?' He sounded surprised.

'Yes, why not?'

'Well. It's the only one that has to be anonymous.'

'That's fine by me.' I said. I had no desire to become well-known as an obituarist.

'Okay,' he said at length, 'Ring up The Times and see if they'll have you do it. I've suggested to Glyn that when we've done our various pieces we should let each other see what's been written – basically to save too much duplication.' This seemed reasonable to me.

After Richard had gone off the telephone, I rang *The Times* and the department dealing with death were happy I should write an obit. on Russell. But they wanted it quickly, no later than the following Sunday – just three days hence. So I set to and, with a little research, I had soon sketched it out. That same evening, Richard was back on the phone to find out if *The Times* had agreed to my doing the obit. I told him they had.

'When do they want it for?'

'The day after tomorrow.'

'That's ridiculous! Why so soon? The man's dead, for God's sake!'

I was unable to enlighten him as to the reason for the rush. Giving a sort of vocal shrug, he rang off, promising to e-mail his obit. when it was ready, and repeating his insistence that I do the same.

Patricia said to me, 'I would never have agreed to send the obit. to him if it had been my choice.'

I looked at my wife in surprise, 'Why ever not?'

'I just wouldn't have, that's all.'

By the following Saturday lunchtime I had written the obituary of Peter Russell; and I had Patricia send it by e-mail to Richard. That evening the telephone sprang into life once more. It was Richard again. He began with the words, 'Yes, it's fine.' I could tell by his tone it wasn't. 'It's just a couple of small things in that second paragraph...'

'What things?' I asked defensively.

'That bit about Peter having nine African wives...'

'He boasted of that, even in print.'

'I know he did. But mention of that...and also the bit about his being a heavy drinker and smoker?'

'He was. Everybody knew he was. If he didn't drink you under the table, he got you with the perpetual incense of his cancer sticks.'

'I know. But I feel it may upset members of his family.'

'He hasn't got much family, has he? Apart from his son in Italy, who must know perfectly well what he was like, and his first wife's dead. His second left him years ago taking the daughters with her to Arkansas or somewhere that's never heard of The Times.'

'I know, but...?'

It was clear by now there were going to be difficulties with this obituary. There were and, in the end, it got considerably altered editorially, and I scarcely recognized it when published.

A few days later, not merely a sanitized version of my obituary of Russell appeared in *The Times,* but a version that had been considerably re-written word for word. The only thing I was glad of was that it was anonymous.

A final little touch to this mysterious reappearance of metaphorical ghosts from the past was a yet further incarnation of Richard Burns who, a few further years on, changed his name to Richard Berengarten. Perhaps to give a fresh start to his poetry writing career?

Some years later, I was again asked to write an obituary – this time of my poet friend Geoffrey Godbert for *The Guardian* newspaper. Apart from writing poems, Geoffrey had been an editor with Anthony Astbury and the playwright Harold Pinter. Together they ran a small press that produced finely printed pamphlets of poetry by the likes of W.S. Graham, George Barker, Hugo Williams and many others. Before he became a famous playwright, Pinter had written poems under the name Harold Pinta. As my father had known Geoffrey's father, he and I met as children and, although we did not meet again until we were both over fifty and continued to meet until the end of his life, I was happy to oblige *The Guardian* with an obituary of Geoffrey. But evidently I had not learned from my earlier experience with *The Times* that there is a greater art to writing obituaries than I had ever dreamed of. Upon publication of Geoffrey's obituary, I received an email (as I believe did the newspaper) from a fellow poet complaining that I had not mentioned him as a friend of Geoffrey's. Naturally I apologised but could do nothing about it as the obituary had already appeared in print. However, although the said poet seemed unaware of the obituary's prior publication when he asked me to change it, he appeared to know what was in it. A foreknowledge similar to that which had arisen with regard to *The Times'* obituary of Peter Russell. Seeing that only *The Guardian's* 'obituaries desk' had had sight of Geoffrey's, I remain unaware of exactly *how* my fellow poet knew what was in it – though poetry and clairvoyance are rumoured to have affinities. Still ... I am now reluctant to indulge further in the art of obituary.

19.
THE CHESSMAN COMETH

Among those who over the years have found their way to The Mount is John Rety. For a long time I knew him only in the context of poetry events such as I have described elsewhere as 'the Unforgettable Torriano'. Brixham being remote from Kentish Town, one never dreamed John would have occasion to come here. But a phone call one day revealed another, less well-known side to our poetry impresario. I have not forgotten how the conversation began:

'Weellium, I haf joost found out Paignton is near where you leeve!'

Not exactly the geographical discovery of the century, but I had to confirm what he said was true. Wondering at the same moment what his interest in the neighbouring town along the bay was. He did not keep me ignorant for long:

'I play the chess at your Oldway Mansion.'

'When?'

'For one week beeginning Sunday.'

It turned out that Paignton – along with the likes of Hastings, Jersey and Gothenberg in Sweden – is a place where chess congresses take place. Further, John was a maestro, a *gross meister*, a chess grand master. It seems, too, there is a famous 'move' or defence in chess called the Rety Something Move; though it seems it was not named after John. Anyway, I suggested we meet up when he came to Torbay; indeed, I invited him to stay at The Mount. It was an offer he readily took up; and the following week he came to us. Each day going off at noon to Oldway Mansion to play chess, returning sometime during the evening dependent on the success or otherwise of the day's game.

John's gift for fueling anecdote is legendary. He even managed a few in Devon. Anyone who has known John Rety for any length of time learns that he is not merely not English (he is, in fact, a Hungarian exile), but he is quite free of the usual constraints that fetter an English adult, male or female. In fact, he is less inhibited than most children; and it is his lack of verbal restraint that is not just touching but astonishing at times. Sometimes one suspects there is an actor lurking in this excitable Eastern European. But John's lack of inhibition can, at times, become something of a strain even to the most tolerant of his friends. And friends with the level of tolerance John needs are not always easy to come by – especially in the ego-ridden world of poetry.

I was once having a drink in a pub with the late Michael Donaghy. We were discussing the business of giving poetry readings. I asked Michael if he had ever read at Torriano. His reply was a sort of hesitant affirmation ('Er, yeah...') followed by, 'This guy Rety invited me to read. Like at many places you sit awhile listening to readings from the audience until like it's your turn to do the guest spot. Anyhow, Rety said he'd introduce me before I did my thing. Which was fair enough. But he began by picking up one of my books, waving it about a bit, and saying in a kind of foreign voice, " The poet who is tonight's guest is...(pause) er..?" He turned the book over like he was proof-reading the cover, and muttering to himself all the time, before finally announcing, "Er, yes, someone called Michael Donaghy...he's American. I haf never heard of heem!" Well, I know I ain't exactly world-famous, but you'd've thought the guy who'd booked me would have remembered my name!' Looking back, of course, I detect a typical touch of Rety subversiveness in his treatment of Donaghy.

John's first visit to The Mount began late one afternoon during a spell of hot weather: warm evenings beneath glistening stars above a faintly murmuring sea, in which we ate out on the front lawn. Carousing and conversing late into the night. Unfortunately, however, the very first day he was with us, John managed to achieve something no one else has managed before in our house; nor indeed elsewhere. As anyone who knows her will tell you, Patricia does not 'lose her cool' easily. But John contrived to quarrel violently with his hostess. I could not believe it. Nobody quarreled with Patricia. But he did. Eventually, they parted company and retired to bed, leaving a somewhat nerve-wracked and nonplused Yours Truly to clear away the dishes, wash them, and ponder late into the night.

The next morning , John appeared up well before Patricia. He said to me (also up early) with a sort of rueful insouciance, 'I sink I haf upset Patreesha, yes?' I agreed he had. He nodded and said, 'I make it up.' And, indeed, make it up he eventually did...somehow.

Although John came to Torbay the following year for the same chess congress, he initially refused to stay with us, accusing me of having led him into too much drinking etc., giving him 'a good time which spoil my game, yes?'

In September 2004 a special double-sized issue of *Acumen* was published to celebrate its 50th number. Patricia and I had just finished dispatching all the subscribers' and contributors' copies in about six-hundred ready stamped envelopes which were collected and taken away by the local postal van. But we still had all the odd-sized packets and parcels for book shops and the like to get dispatched when John and his partner Susan came to stay. To do the final dispatching it meant dragging a large grip and a shopping trolley down to the general post office in the town centre where the packets would be weighed and posted.

The evening before this final dispatching of the most bulky issue ever of the magazine our friends arrived. They were to stay for the chess week. We had insisted Susan came with John this time as it would give her a holiday by the sea while he was out playing chess. And so it proved: Patricia, Susan and I had a lot of fun of our own while the maestro spent his days working out the mathematics of a million moves in the grand Victorian portals of Oldway Mansion, Paignton.

After an early breakfast the next day, John volunteered to help me get the collection of parcels to the post office in Brixham. Patricia was having to stay at home for a delivery of something, and John nobly offered to accompany me in her place.

On arriving at the post office we found a queue of some four or five people outside the entrance waiting for the office to open. Inwardly, I groaned, because I recognized two somewhat eccentric figures at the head of the queue who were regular customers with an enormous ability to gossip in public places. And the thought of John getting drawn into their verbal circle was, to say the least, a disquieting prospect. However, he abruptly became distracted from paying attention to them.

Fore Street, on which the Brixham main post office is situated, is a not-very-wide thoroughfare that is now pedestrianized for much of the day. John was gazing down the street in the direction of the harbour. Coming towards us was a young woman of perhaps 25 years of age. A gypsy-like figure, she was lightly clad, indeed revealingly so: a voluptuous being with long dark hair, large earrings, and a great sun tan. She had a large dog on a lead pulling her along. As this sensual apparition drew level with the queue outside the post office, John suddenly exclaimed in a loud voice that attracted everyone within hearing and mortified me: '*Oh*, yes! *Oh*, yes!' (In his mildly foreign accent it came over as 'Orryezz!, Orryezz!')

Startled, the girl looked towards us and half-smiled; but without stopping. Immediately, gesturing after her, John turned to me: 'You see that? She smile at me! You know why?'

'I, er...?'

'She smile at me because she know I admire her dog!'

I stared at John in disbelief. However, I had no time to digest further this hitherto unknown fact of his worship of canine pulchritude, before a second 'incident' occurred. And a potentially more difficult one.

Adjacent to the entrance to the post office was a small, low bench capable of seating no more than three persons. There suddenly appeared on this bench a body-pierced, tattoo'd young man in vest and shorts. With him was a thin, rather timid-looking skinny blonde, doubtless his girl friend. Seated, they were no more than a yard or two away from John and myself. Suddenly, the skinhead's mobile phone rang and he answered it. At which John began a denunciatory speech about the dangers of mobile phone usage and its effect upon the ears and the brain. 'Eet scrambles your brain! Eet make you completely stupid!' he cried in the young man's direction, telling me and the rest of the queue at the same time. So loud did John get that the young man couldn't hear himself speak and had to cross to the other side of the street to better continue his telephone conversation.

I thought, 'Oh, God, we're in for trouble now!' As soon as the skinhead had finished his call he was bound to come across the road and thump John, I felt certain. And there was I weighed down with all those damn parcels! However, just at that moment, the post office opened its doors and the queue filed in. Once inside – in fact, after we had been inside a few minutes, but before we had reached the counter to be served – John turned to me and said, 'You know what to do. I leave you now. I look round the town.' And with that he marched out of the post office.

About a quarter of an hour later, the parcels having been stamped-up and dispatched, I emerged from the building. After sometime, I found my companion – totally unscathed – staring in what we call in Devon 'a grock shop' window – that is to say John was staring in the window of a souvenir shop, a happy expression on his small, bearded face.

For all the hassle – real or potential – that John Rety can involve one in, somehow one forgives him. I think it is because – as our Brixham friend, David Beugger once put it – 'You realize there is a warmth, a real humanity in Rety.'

In the summer when John came a third time alone, and for the last time, he began to accuse me of having led him astray with drink and pipe-smoking (I smoked a pipe then). He would return to The Mount in a big sulk. And one evening, when he came back late and David Beugger and I were sat drinking at the table on the front lawn, David asked him courteously how his game had gone that afternoon. Rety looked back over his shoulder as he flashed past us and climbed to the front door, and shouted 'Vot is it to yoo?' Then he disappeared upstairs to the guest room and did not appear for an hour or more.

Warmth…humanity or whatever, yes, John Rety could be a very difficult person. I vividly recall an evening at the Torriano Meeting House (so called because it had once been a Quaker meeting place) when a man, driven to exasperation by Rety's comments, suddenly picked up John bodily and slammed him against the wall outside, waving his fist in Rety's face. I had to intercede to calm them both down.

Despite everything however, I made some good friends at the Torriano readings. Friends like Arthur Jacobs, the shyest poet I ever knew; and at Torriano I first met Danielle Hope and David Perman, whom I had only known as correspondents hitherto. Danielle, in her student years at Nottingham University had run a poetry magazine called *Zenos*; and I have spoken of David Perman elsewhere. There, too, did I re-encounter the poet and translator Dinah Livingstone, whom I had not seen since when, as a teenager, she had performed her poems at the Lamb & Flag readings in Covent Garden. Eventually, Danielle became advisory editor to Patricia's magazine *Acumen* – a long-standing friendship that has never faltered through her generosity which included providng the magazine with a sub-office at her London home. But this is all just to acknowledge that though the chess maestro could be very difficult at times, Patricia and I owe much to him, to his partner Susan (the power behind the throne?) and their daughter Emily.

20.
A FRIEND IN NEED

A few years ago our friends John and Gina got married in Cheltenham at the local registry office. They had a fine celebration for many friends at their home after the ceremony. It was at the latter I first properly met Roy Davids, the former head of the manuscripts' department at Sotheby's. Although I had encountered his name on a number of occasions because of his business connection with John, I had only once met him years before, and then only fleetingly. The place was John's flat in Wigmore Street and the sole thing I can recall of the encounter was that, when he had departed, John informed me that Roy had recently 'had open-heart surgery'.

At our second encounter, however, I learned a number of other things about Roy, as well as forming a fairly quick appreciation of his gift of charming and intelligent conversation. I learned that he was both a collector of poetical manuscripts, of ceramics, and of paintings, as well as being a dealer in manuscripts. In fact, from what he said, he had made a considerable amount of money as a dealer. Additionally, for some fifteen years he had been Poet Laureate, Ted Hughes's agent for the sale of manuscripts, letters and notebooks both of Hughes' and his dead wife the poet and feminist icon Sylvia Plath. It was at that point, too, he informed me, with sudden but understandable solemnity, that 'Ted has cancer...but only a few people know.' Then, while I was digesting this piece of confidentiality, he abruptly changed the subject to inform me, in way of a compliment, that he had read a poem of mine which he liked very much. It was a poem I had written about a cottage near Burford where the newly-married couple had lived before setting up home in Cheltenham: a cottage which evidently Roy knew. Anyway, in the years succeeding this occasion, Patricia and I got to know Roy better, and entertained him on occasion at The Mount, as well as having been his guest in Great Haseley village near Oxford.

A year or two after our stay at his house in Great Haseley, Roy came to visit us in Devon and began by telling us his latest great secret which 'you must keep to yourselves'. What this secret amounted to was that he had spent more than six months cataloguing yet another famous but deceased poet's archive that was important because it would 'dispel many of the myths surrounding this poet once it is in the public domain'. Roy, of course, was a well-known and respected cataloguer of manuscripts, etc. Unfortunately, however, the effort of the cataloguing of this collection had left him distinctly unwell, his back paining him so much that he could hardly walk at all.

Given that two years before he had embarked upon selling his large collection of paintings, prints and sketches of famous poets – which had, itself, been a work-intensive undertaking, but had resulted in a sale amounting to many hundreds of thousands of pounds – it surprised us that he should have immediately undertaken a further equally arduous task. To Patricia and me it hardly seemed that he needed the money. Was it worth his now having made himself ill with this second great effort?

At first, both he and we thought he was merely suffering the effects of stress. But, some days after he went back home, Roy informed us by phone that he was submitting himself to a thorough medical examination. What that would discover he did not know; but would we come and visit him in a few weeks' time? This we agreed to do, hoping that by the time we went to stay with him the cause of his medical problem would have been discovered. And, indeed, by the time we went to stay with him, it had been discovered that the artificial aorta, which had been implanted in him all those years before, was no longer functioning properly, and a fresh bout of open-heart surgery would have to be undergone. Our sojourn with him that weekend was dominated by two things: his impending operation, and the huge, brooding pile of papers and files of the great dead poet on the floor of his library. A man of fastidious tidiness, Roy's house was beginning to betray signs of neglect: proof of his ill-health. And further proof of that indisposition was to manifest itself soon also.

As the time drew near for his operation at the beginning of November, he would ring Patricia up with increasing frequency simply for someone to talk to. John and Gina also would get regular calls from him; as, doubtless, would other friends we knew nothing of. One of the things he would talk to Patricia about was his (and her) idea for an anthology of poetry culled from the first sixty issues of *Acumen*. There was much talk of this during the weeks leading up to his operation until it was abruptly shelved for two reasons. Firstly, Patricia became totally involved in preparations for the day-to-day running of the 6th Torbay Poetry Festival in late October; and, secondly, Roy, having decided he might die on the operating table, set about writing his will. Something that John Wilson confirmed who went to see Roy – by then incarcerated in the John Radcliffe Hospital in Oxford – who, when John offered to bring him any books or newspapers he might want, retorted that he was 'too busy writing my will to read anything else'.

However, some months on, the Torbay Poetry Festival behind us, and Roy's operation having been successfully carried out (save for the major hiccup of an almost immediate second op. because his metal stitches failed to work properly), we were soon back in touch with him. Only it was a Roy become manic through drugs and post-operative stress: one who couldn't stop talking over the telephone, and was full of grandiose schemes – especially for poetry. Having written some interesting poems himself – something of a revelation to himself – it had led him to the feeling of having undergone a 'Road to Damascus' conversion. With the result his declared intention was to devote his fortune to doing things tangible for the Muse, ranging from giving his fine collection of poetry books and manuscripts to the Bodleian Library, to helping finance the proposed *Acumen* anthology. 'But', said he. 'as I may die under the knife, I am including all these financial proposals in the will I am writing'. Like I say, however, he did not die. And despite whatever he may, or may not, have put in his will, as soon as the operations were over, he sent Patricia a cheque towards financing the proposed anthology. Something which amused me greatly because, some time back, I had asked him if he would like to buy an advance copy (fifteen quid) of the fine limited edition of my booklet *Poems Antibes*, to which he had replied in the negative, saying he'd 'wait until they appeared in a collected poems of Oxley', which he felt assured they eventually would. Like so many of my male friends who will never confront Patricia with anything critical, Roy had learnt to seize any opportunity to get in little digs at me, usually verbal, but this was a fifteen pound, or if one prefers, a five thousand pound dig at me! (Not only Roy could show signs of paranoia, let it be noted!)

The next stage in this poetic and medical saga was that Roy summoned us to visit him in Oxford. But not at the John Radcliffe Hospital, rather at a hotel called The Old Bank in the High. He had transferred himself there as soon as possible in order to convalesce and to be near his own GP's surgery ('over a wine shop!'), and to have a degree of freedom he would not have enjoyed in a convalescent home. He told us to come first-class by train, at his expense, and 'a car will meet you at Oxford Station'.

No car met us at the station; but neither did we travel first-class: which was fortunate seeing that, on arrival, he blandly informed us 'you should charge it as a business expense', meaning, of course, against the non-profit-making and non-profitable magazine Patricia runs. We took a taxi to this highly-expensive hotel; and although we got no breakfast the next morning, we were treated to a good meal on arrival in our bedroom where we spent many hours talking about the projected anthology, about Roy's desire to have a book of his own poetry, and many more matters poetic besides. Also, despite Roy's injunction at the moment of our arrival interdicting discussion of his health and operation, from time to time he would sidetrack his more intellectual monologue to speak of his recent medical experiences. But, of course, the clearly stressed often mimic the logic of the autocrat.

As I say, we were treated to a fine meal that evening; though not in the hotel's sumptuous dining room because, 'Even in the non-smoking section I can detect smoke and I don't want to cough'. Nevertheless, much of Roy's evening was punctuated by bouts of coughing, due to his incessant talking, but that's another matter, I guess. I was especially pleased to be made at my ease right from our arrival by Roy's summoning of his Polish servant-waiter whom he ordered to bring me a large glass of first-rate red wine 'every 20 minutes' (to Patricia's dismay, which was not diminished much by the glasses of champagne he ordered for her: though the wine proved of such good quality, I experienced neither inebriation nor other side-effects such as a hangover the following day).

The next morning we received an internal call from Roy, politely demanding our presence in his room for 8.15am. Our discourse of the preceding evening continued apace, only this time considerably spiced-up by the news that, 'because of a certain woman psycho-therapist, I am to be interviewed by two eminent psychiatrists with a view to having me sectioned'. According to our friend some years ago, after he had left Sotheby's, he had gone into a deep depression. To try to get out of this, Roy had voluntarily placed himself in the hands of a woman psycho-therapist. Eventually, she had rescued him from his Slough of Despond and he had been very grateful to her, going on, 'to become friends with her and her husband socially'. But, after the second part of his recent operation for a new aorta, Roy had once again slumped in a trough of depression; and although he had not seen this woman for about three years, he nevertheless rang her up for help. His specific request was for her to come to the hospital and sit with him through the worst of the nights after he had recovered consciousness. This she had declined to do but had come to visit him during daylight visiting hours. After having some talk with the patient, and staying with Roy a while, he claimed she had gone and told the hospital authorities that, in her professional opinion, such was his state of mind he should be examined by the hospital's consultant psychiatrists, 'With a view to having me sectioned...declared insane!' he repeated. Roy then added that not only had this woman seen the hospital doctors about him, but she had actually contacted 'the great poet's wife and warned her I was not of sound mind!' This had led the poet's widow and executor to request the return of all the poet's material. Last, and perhaps least, of the information Roy gave us concerning his prospective 'sectioning' was to tell us he was insisting his lawyer be present at this interview with the hospital's two consultant psychiatrists. 'For I've just got to get this woman off my back.' Amongst the other pieces of information that our friend let slip was the woman's name, though he had said he wouldn't, and the fact that she 'wrote poetry but never revised it, something I told her she should do if she expected it to be any good.' Neither Patricia nor I had ever heard of this supposed woman poet; but it hardly mattered in the light of all the other information Roy had given us.

Roy to be sectioned? It was a ridiculous notion. Both Patricia and I had known poets, whose eyes would, from time to time, 'in a fine frenzy roll', but that was normal with poets. Yes, to complete the Shakespeare quote, 'Poets, lovers, madmen' are 'of a single imagination all compact'. Near allied, but a poet is rarely a lunatic. There was nothing in Roy's flights of fancy that were not normal in a poet. As for the psycho-therapist's claim he was having delusions of grandeur, maybe he was, but that certainly does not prove a person to be a genuine madman. Besides, it was still so near the time of the major surgery he had undergone that it was positively obscene to consider a formal investigation of his state of sanity. Who would not be distressed for some while after having such an operation? Who would not be likely to suffer false euphoria when pumped full of post-operative drugs? There seemed both an element of absurdity and unreality in what was developing around our friend. But what could Patricia and I do about it? What do to help? Nothing, really, save stay in touch and keep informed of what happened.

At precisely 9.45am we were dismissed from Roy's appropriately royal presence. After checking out of the hotel, we spent a quiet day looking round Oxford, before going out to Boar's Hill to stay overnight with Tony and Fran. As they knew Roy slightly through us, there was much discussion in the evening, and the next day before we returned to Brixham, discussion about the Case of Roy. Tony was amazed at the seeming drama of it all, and kept shaking his head and saying, 'Sectioned? It's hard to believe', and indeed it was. And, in the end it did not happen. But the Great Poet's archive was speedily returned to his widow; and Roy did not seem unhappy, despite the fact he estimated its worth as considerable, 'which means that the she devil has lost me a potential commission of many thousands of pounds...as well as a good friend in the poet's widow.'

Speaking of money, Roy confessed that the inventory he had had to make for the writing of his will had shown 'I am far richer than I thought I was'. Consequently, it crossed both my mind and Patricia's – albeit fleetingly – that, somehow, money might be at the bottom of much of what was going on. The root of all evil?

21.
NAME-DROPPING

As this year is the hundredth anniversary of Auden's birth I took a couple of his volumes off one of my shelves and noticed they were both signed. This took me back to the occasion when he signed them – a dog-eared copy of his Penguin Selected and a first edition of *City Without Walls* – sometime in the late Sixties or early Seventies. But before I describe the event, as I shall, it occurred to me that as I never knew Auden personally, anything I might say would only look like a pretext for name-dropping. And although I have known many a great name-dropper in the poetry world – all poets do it at some time or other as one learns – I can never get out of my head what Somerset Maughan said of the habit, 'name-dropping is an embarrassing habit because it seems something of a confession as to what a nonentity one is compared to those whose names one mentions implying acquaintance'. I paraphrase, not having the text to hand, but it occurs, I think, in one of his essays on literature or in the foreword to something else he wrote. So writing with that in mind, I hope it will be allowed that my presumption in this matter is motivated not by any desire to add to my own self-importance, but simply by the wish to commit to paper a few thoughts engendered by the memory of hearing Auden read his poetry; and by having spent a short period in his presence in a bookshop: a presence somewhat magisterial if a little down-at-heel.

The reading took place, not inappropriately for Auden, in a church – probably Anglican given his belief in later life – St. George's in Bloomsbury Way, London's West End. As I recall it, it was a somewhat dark and faded edifice both inside and out that perfectly matched the crumpled, brown-suited figure with multi-lined visage who read his work in a sort of crunchy monotone voice. It was dark evening when the reading began and the church was not much more than dimly lit. However, there was a goodly poetic congregation en-pewed to hear this famous poet best associated with the political Thirties. But a poet also, like any good poet, who was the author of a handful (it is rarely more than that) of anthologisable 'gems' of the sort that any Palgrave worth his salt would pick up. Though none of these, as I recall, did he read that evening, concentrating on more recent work, especially that contained in *City Without Walls*, which he was then promoting, and others which were collected later in his final volume *Thank You Fog*. I have to say that, though I was interested to hear him read, I was not as *au fait* with his work as I later became: something which was largely because, at that time, I was most wrapped up in the work of Eliot and Pound and the other principal modernists.

After the reading was over, a goodly proportion of Auden's audience trooped around the corner to Francis Long's bookshop in Museum Street an independent bookshop now long gone (no pun intended, though Auden would have appreciated it believing 'Good poets love bad puns'). Once in this well-lighted bookshop, people purchased copies of *City Without Walls* and queued up to get Auden's signature. Two things I recall from that wait were that a man called John Whitehead, whom I had briefly met from another part of my life, startled Auden by producing what appeared to me like a play script but was, in fact, a rare copy in mint condition of the book of Auden's poems published at Oxford by his friend Stephen Spender in the 1920's. Its owner wished for Auden's signature on it and, having signed it, Auden remarked that before he signed it, it had been 'worth at least a thousand' but now 'you may double that.' But of more interest to me was the moment I handed him my copy of *City Without Walls* which he signed then, to my surprise, opened the book and turned to one of the poems to correct a line or misprint. In those days it just had never occurred to me that, once a poem was published in a book, it could be changed. Later, I learned that Robert Graves would indulge in the wholesale revision of poems between each new Selected or Collected edition of his work. And I once took a book of Dannie Abse's poems off a shelf in his house to peruse and was astonished to find several of the poems extensively altered by hand.

So that was how I acquired W.H. Auden's monica on one of my copies of his poems; I think the other was signed at a later occasion at the Royal Festival Hall after another reading. In early 1972 I had embarked on the business of editing a small magazine called *Littack*. I was also by that time very familiar with other little literary and poetry magazines – very many of which then, as now, were littering 'the Scene', as it was often referred to. And frequently I encountered poems by Auden. It seemed that this very famous poet was quite happy to appear in such limited circulation journals, as well as in prestigious periodicals like *The New Yorker* or *The Times Literary Supplement*. I did not then know the reason for this, it being some years before I learned that many established poets of those days liked to keep in touch with the little magazine world because they often had started in such places themselves. Today though, winning poetry competitions or being short-listed for them, has become more important than little magazine publication. The poets of earlier times felt that it would be helpful to the appreciation of their own poetry, as well as offering examples of quality work to aspiring poets, to still support such independent publications. As Dannie Abse once put it memorably to me, 'When I was a young aspiring poet it was the understood practice of older, more established poets to show kindness to beginners.' The context of this remark, I have to record, was made with reference to an older and famous poet who had *not* been helpful or kind to Dannie as a young unknown poet. But, almost always, senior poets took it as their duty to encourage tyro versifiers. And, as much as anything, this was owing to the fact that poetry was then still seen as a vocation and had yet to become a career: though the notion of the career poet cannot have been entirely without foundation in fact because, for example, Robert Graves often spoke dismissively of 'career poets'. In America, where poetry had begun entering academia from the late Forties onwards, doubtless the term had greater substance, with the consequence that a poet's social and other efforts were likely to be, in some degree at least, directed towards career advancement, and except within the context of the classroom (where students, in any case, paid for advice and tuition) an established poet was much less inclined to share his or her time with unknowns in the field of poetry.

Not so the likes of Robert Graves, Kathleen Raine or Hugh MacDiarmid and others with whom I corresponded as a young poet. And Auden too. Though I regret I had not written to him earlier than the summer of 1973 asking for a poem to grace the pages of my magazine. His reply was, yes, I could have one provided I 'could offer a small fee' as poetry was what he made his living by. Unfortunately, when his letter came I was on holiday, so I could not respond to it immediately. But when I returned home and was preparing to reply to him, I heard on the radio that he had died in a Vienna hotel. So that was that. Auden made his living by writing but he was no careerist. Today, of course, things are different like I say.

22.
THE ULTIMATE REMOVAL

My friend Beugger – yes, that's 'bugger' with a random 'e' thrown in – was the principal eccentric in my (and Patricia's) life. Once, before the onset of real old age, he was about six feet two in height and of a solid build; and there is no better way to describe him than as a superannuated Viking. This latter because, though born in Naples of a supposedly Scottish mother and a Swiss father, he was of Norwegian descent, hence his full nomenclatures, namely, 'John, David, *Erik, Knud,* Beugger'. A man congenitally idle, he nevertheless possessed a gene of great strength that was totally unaffected by lack of any exercise. As for the 'superannuated' bit, that not only emphasized his Oblamov-like commitment to inactivity but, also, that after failing to hold down many an indifferent job, he ended up being retired prematurely from the Bankruptcy Department of the Civil Service on a much-reduced pension. However, due to apparently adequate supplies of that commodity known as 'private income', he never seemed deprived of life's comforts.

I have described our friend as eccentric. A simple word but one covering even more complexity than either his ancestry or his finances. Before he swam into our ken, he'd had two nervous breakdowns that had left him with Obsessive Compulsive Disorders. I should mention the most persistent one first, only because it was the one that people noticed, his obsession with latrines. His whole day was punctuated by frequent and often lengthy sojourns in toilets: regularly to the great inconvenience of others who might wish to avail themselves of the same facility (especially where there was only a single WC, which is often the case in private houses). Equally irritating to friends or acquaintances, he could never leave a place without visiting the 'loo first. Of course, like Lady Macbeth, such visits involved much ridiculously excessive hand-washing.

While another of his quirks lay in what I would term 'door stroking': his habit of checking and fondling and rattling doors to see they were properly closed, something which did, in fact, result in damage through wear-and-tear to many doors. For a time he had worked in a laboratory despite the fact that he had a mortal fear of chemicals – especially anything he thought might be poisonous. And, wherever he lived he would never have gas in the house in case it blew him up. He had a blood phobia too. Blood meant death to him. He suffered, too, from acute vertigo. There are three steps to our front door: descending them made him feel noticeably nervous.

But the chief problem created by such OCD was it soon betrayed the overriding fact that Beugger was completely inflexible in his habits and could not accommodate himself to others' timetables. With the result that, over time, he had never retained any friends, either male or female, save ourselves.

On two occasions in his life he made it his business to take up residence near to where we lived. The first occasion was when we lived at Epping in Essex: Beugger came and resided in nearby Buckhurst Hill. Then, when we decamped to South Devon, he eventually – after an interval of more than twenty years – followed us to Brixham. The reasons for the big interlude was that he had moved up north to live with his aging mother; though, from time to time, he would descend upon us for holidays. This, despite the fact that he had initially strongly disapproved of our move to Brixham, giving it as his opinion that we would 'grow tired eventually of the cloying beauty of the area'. Nonetheless, in 1999 on the death of his mother, he came to live permanently in Brixham.

At first, he was 'demob happy', lavishing money on us, and any of our friends who came to stay with us. In addition, we included him in a whole range of social events both within the bay and elsewhere: often taking him on literary jaunts to London (he stayed himself at the Civil Service Club in Whitehall), and to elsewhere like Edinburgh or Paris. Unfortunately, however, after a while he felt that he could no longer stand the pace of our lifestyle; nor was he happy that it was costing him so much.

Now, two further things need to be appreciated about David. First, and of less importance in the initial years in Devon than it subsequently became, was the fact that we knew him to be a dedicated valetudinarian, but only latterly appreciated that he was, also, a monstrous hypochondriac. Additionally, he was an enormous pessimist who expected everything to turn out for the bad. These things tended to weary Patricia and I a little, but we felt loyalty to someone who had clung to us so long: the barnacle and the rock must eventually become tolerant of one another.

Second, and of more immediate concern, was his contradictory attitude to money. For years he had convinced us, by his financial generosity, that he was munificent not mean. Yet, at the same time, he always banged the drum of thrift...at least verbally. But like all self-deluding persons, David was a big liar. On innumerable occasions he had been caught out by Patricia and me lying to us, and always he had tried – usually with practised disingenuousness – to further lie his way out. So, eventually, I decided to inquire a bit more into his financial affairs. Accidentally, I discovered that another of his OCD's was costing him over £2,000 per year. This was his psychotic obsession with hoarding everything that came his way rather like a human magpie. We knew, of course, that in his little room at the Smuggler's Haunt Hotel he kept hundreds of unnecessary things from carrier bags to old newspapers, plus any junk mail and every single bill he had received for anything he purchased, etc. But of more costly significance was the discovery that he was paying a storage depot in Gateshead to keep the entire contents of the bungalow he had vacated on his mother's death, most of which possessions he would clearly never need as he hoped to see out his days in his already crowded room in the hotel, having no wish ever to look after himself if it could be avoided. Eventually, Patricia got him to admit there really was no purpose in his paying such a yearly rental to retain a mass of unwanted things in a warehouse. And the upshot was that she made arrangements – Beugger signing letters she had written in his name – to get his northern chattels transferred to the nearest depot of Pickfords, to Exeter.

In due course, four huge containers were brought to a depot in Exeter, and arrangements were made for Patricia and Beugger to go to there with a view to disposing of most things either by auction, by sending them to the public landfill site, or by bringing books and more personal things that he wished to keep to Brixham. With regard to the books, and knowing how little space he had available at the hotel, I offered him an empty bookcase in my vestibule, and another in the hallway, for him to keep his books. 'Would that be enough space for your books?' I had asked. 'Oh, more than enough!' he assured me.

Two days then ensued that were crucial to this removal. The first was the expedition he and Patricia made to the Exeter depot. On the day in question, Beugger and she traveled to Exeter, and in a frenzy of activity driven by Patricia, everything was examined from paintings, furniture, silverware to back copies of the *Nature* magazine (Beugger having once been, as I said, an analytical chemist), half-opened boxes of Kellogg's corn flakes, innumerable old tins, hundreds of carrier bags, empty egg boxes, old invoices going back to the 1950's, and a multitude of things both useful and manifestly useless. Anyway, the upshot was that some of it was eventually sold at auction for almost a thousand pounds, quite a lot of things went to charity shops, a great mound of useless junk went to a landfill site, and those things that Beugger wished especially to keep, or to make gifts of to friends, were collected together for transportation to Brixham in due course.

It was arranged that the storage firm would first visit The Smuggler's Haunt to deliver one portion of the goods, the carrier being met by Beugger and Patricia. After dropping off there, the van would then come to The Mount with Beugger's books where I would be waiting. It was a pleasant day, sunny and warm, so I sat on the bench in the front garden reading a book. The carrier was supposed to call at The Smuggler's Haunt at around 10.30pm., and when they'd unloaded there Patricia would let me know they were on their way. But having not heard from her by 11 o'clock, I rang her only to discover that the carrier had not shown up so far. Minutes later, however, a large white van began to back up our lane. It was the carrier; and it turned out that they – two blokes – had decided to reverse the order of dropping off. So I rang Patricia and said they had arrived and would be with her and Beugger shortly.

Very soon there was a great pyramid of boxes on the front lawn of 6 The Mount, together with sundry other items including a camping stove, a microwave oven and a fridge. Surely this lot couldn't be for storage at our house? Yes, as it turned out, the fridge was for Patricia; and the brand new microwave was for Beugger's goddaughter, our daughter Kate. But all those other boxes marked *Books*? Surely there were far more than Beugger had thought he had got. So I insisted on opening a few. Books were, indeed, in the first box unloaded. But the second box with identical marking in fact contained a ridiculous number of miniature radios. While a third had an electric fire, a drill and set of screwdrivers, plus more torches than I had ever seen in one place together. *Books* indeed!

At this point I was distracted by the men carrying the fridge and demanding to know where it was to be put. We have our freezer – soon to be joined by said fridge – in the shed at the side of our house. Fitting the new fridge in beside the freezer was not easy! It involved much bending, sweating and swearing by the deliverers. Then I rang Patricia at The Smuggler's Haunt to let her know the men were on their way down to her.

I proceeded to busy myself opening all the boxes in turn. I soon discovered that though a few more contained things in no way describable as books (hedge clippers, trowel, shovel, fork and such like) there were, nevertheless, many boxes of books as well. A considerable quantity of, in fact, numbering many, many more than Beugger had assured me there would be. I set to and began furiously filling the two bookcases I had assigned him from my library, only to find how little space there was for his books. I then carried all the boxes round the side of the house and covered them up again with the plastic ground sheet. It was obvious that, at some later date, David would have to come up to our house and engage in yet another sorting and disposal of his too many accumulated possessions. Brixham's charity shops were in for a bonanza if they but knew it!

The many subsequent days Patricia spent trying to help digest into Beugger's life the consequence of this removal were both heroic and trying. I leant what assistance I could, but she carried the main burden. Such sayings as 'No, David, you do not need seven suitcases at all!' and 'A 1965 rates' bill is not a memento worth keeping.' And 'What tablets are these?' Beugger, 'My mother's.' 'But, David, she's been dead for three years, so why are you keeping them?' I kept saying consolingly to a frenzied Beugger, 'At least it's saved you a couple of thousand quid in storage rental?'

Death occurred for our friend on 29th December 2007. But, before adding a short appendix on this event, it is necessary to briefly advert to yet another 'removal' in his life. Several years after the first removal already described, the then owners of The Smuggler's Haunt decided to sell up and emigrate to New Zealand. However, by that time Beugger – the hotel's only permanent guest – had become something of an embarrassment to the hotel on account of his overcrowded room that no chambermaid was allowed to clean. Something that would be an impediment to the sale of the hotel. The departing owners of the hotel, however, neatly solved the problem by moving Beugger to a small and pleasant flat immediately opposite The Smuggler's Haunt. This meant that, though sleeping elsewhere than the hotel, he could continue uninterruptedly to take all his meals at the hotel, spending his evenings in the bar enjoying the conviviality and gossip of the place. Fortunately, this removal proved far less traumatic than the first. Though once again it did involve Patricia in a deal of work.

It is no part of this chapter to tell of Beugger's last days. But one or two additional facts are necessary, if not to shed further light upon his character, at least to add to his human mystery.

Over the years Beugger had been drawn into our various poetry ventures. In the early Seventies he went into partnership with Patricia and me to found The Ember Press which has always been, as it were, the holding partnership for all our publishing ventures. His part in the partnership ended when we moved to Brixham and I repaid him his capital investment of £250. After he moved to Brixham, he became a sponsor of Patricia's Torbay Poetry Festival from its second year onwards and joined its committee; though this was only a notional, not a financial sponsorship, he merely giving his time to the festival. He was, of course, completely useless at executing any task; but all agreed it was nice to have him around and, without fail, he always voted the same way as Patricia. He was, however, good at one thing.

Serving 'on the door' at various poetry festival events with Danny Pyle, a fellow committee member, David proved uncharacteristically adroit at preventing people sneaking in for free. His wonderful gentlemanly charm, that was a veritable parody of the idea of a gentleman, never failed to work with the fair sex of any age above 15 years; under that age he simply resorted to bribery with sweets, chocolate and ice cream. Also, he himself having an inordinate love of ice cream, an offer of some to him was the one thing in life that could interrupt and delay one of his innumerable visits to the lavatory. Anyway, his nine years living at or near to The Smuggler's Haunt, and his slightly lesser period with The Torbay Poetry Festival meant that, including his favourite taxi driver, a nurse from the hospice with which he was connected towards the end of his life, and the new proprietors of the hotel, there were about a dozen poetry friends plus a few other acquaintances at his cremation in Torquay, followed by a wake at the Smuggler's Haunt.

It was generally agreed that the ceremony at the crematorium, and the wake afterwards, were agreeable and sensitive occasions that revealed a real warmth of feeling towards the departed. More specifically, the warmth of feeling *and* the continued puzzlement over this outstanding but terribly flawed character were further demonstrated, even amplified at the wake. This latter occurred when one of the guests – a man in his late sixties called Keith, a regular in the hotel bar – told us of his firm belief that Beugger had been, in fact, not your ordinary retired civil servant at all but a government spy, 'probably MI6'. Patricia and I who had known Beugger so much longer than anyone; who thought, at the very least, we knew all about his life, if not about his confused character; we who were always well aware of his many lies; nonetheless we were dumbfounded to hear this. I felt it to be a colourful lie too far. I asked Keith what proof he had of his assertion. Said Keith, 'One evening, some years back, he showed us his passports – he had several, one was in Swiss, I think; or maybe Italian – anyway. One of them showed that, immediately after the war, he was traveling back and forth from France on a regular basis.' There was nothing to say to this, other than it came as great surprise to both Patricia and myself.

Some days later, however, still thinking of our late friend – whom I once dubbed 'a great confusionist' on the grounds that he had an outstanding talent for both giving and taking 'the wrong end of the stick' – I vaguely recalled a conversation of many years ago. The burden of the conversation was – though at that moment I recalled few details – that, when Beugger and his mother and sister had lived in Esher, Surrey, a neighbour of theirs, who often visited them, had been somehow implicated in the great spy scandal connected with the Krogers, who gave atomic secrets to the Russians in the late Forties. So may be there had been more to our friend than even had met our eyes...in all those years leading up to the ultimate removal of all. Ah, well, anything had to be possible with a man, who being on a coach trip to Italy, when half way up Mount Etna, rushed down again to 'find a Gents'!

Later, discussing with our daughter Elizabeth this aspect of the Beugger mystery, she made an interesting observation. Said she: 'Well, it could explain one thing. If he really had been a spy...and been tortured...that would certainly explain all his many hang-ups, wouldn't it?' Patricia and I reflected on this suggestion for some time. Beugger *tortured?* Well, yes, that certainly would explain so much. But we would never know.

Finally, I have often wondered how to describe this man physically, and still the only succinct phrase I ever came up with was as I said at the start of this chapter, especially in his middle years, he resembled 'a superannuated Viking'. I still think that was a true description of this tall, lean, abnormally strong fair-haired man (who was always convinced of his physical feebleness). As for his puzzling, infuriating ways of thinking, his mental attitude: though Patricia and I loved him dearly, he was, undoubtedly, the only person we ever met who gave 'lateral thinking' a bad name.

23.
THE BIRTHDAY PARTY

Not Harold Pinter's but Alan Brownjohn's. At The North Star pub in Swiss Cottage. A perfect poets' pub. Which is not to say a pub for perfect poets, for there are none, but one possessed of a slightly shabby, first floor function room with gloomy bar. The editor of *Acumen* and I decided, having received an invite to Alan's 75th birthday bash, coinciding with the publication of a new collected poems for him, that we'd pay a lightning visit to the metropolis, meeting up with the magazine's advisory editor, Danielle Hope, stay overnight with her and go to the party. Not the first time we've made one of these 24 hour 'flying visits' to a literary function in London, only this time the flying visit was also a frying visit, the temperature being an unusual, globally-warmed 36 degrees centigrade. The sad bit first, however.

We called in at St. Mary's hospital near Paddington Station to visit John Heath-Stubbs, having been apprised of his having pneumonia by Leah Fritz. We found him lying in a semi-foetal position, wearing a nappy and nightshirt, on a bed in an over-hot ward called Thistlethwaite. Nearly ninety years of age, I was reminded of the late James Brockway's cruel but accurate comment about the many photographs taken of Heath-Stubbs, England's premier blind bard, to whit, 'Why do they always make him in photos look like a propped-up corpse?' Now, in that bed, this giant of a man, shrunk to Belsen-like proportions, looked like a corpse lying down. He had also lost much of his hearing, so that it was difficult, at first, to get through to him who we were. It turned out that the pitch of Patricia's voice could be apprehended by him better than mine so that, for the first time in all our encounters with him, she did most of the talking, I just prompting her with a few questions. Though his body had mostly withered away, the almost permanent insomnia of his tremendously memoried brain meant that, in place of tiredness, he had only boredom.

Sad, too, after we'd taken a long, slow stroll to Swiss Cottage on leaving John; and stopping off for a lime and soda and bowl of chips at the first-floor Wetherspoon's diner-pub overlooking the Finchley Road, the first person we sat with at Alan's party was Dannie Abse whose opening words were about an article which had appeared in *The Western*

Mail. It was the account of the car crash last year near Porthcawl in which Dannie had been injured and his wife, our dear friend Joan, had died. In the post at home, just as we were leaving to get the train from Paignton, the newspaper cutting about the inquest had come from Glyn Pursglove in Swansea. I had decided to leave it at home for Patricia to read after we had returned. Said Dannie, 'This journalist rang me up about it. I wasn't at the inquest, but it apparently quotes me...It was the statement I gave to the police at the time. I haven't seen the article myself.' I told him I had, because Glyn had sent it to us. 'Would you send me a copy. I think I ought to see it.' He didn't add, 'I was in the accident too, you know?', but he might as well have. I promised I would send him a copy of the piece. But I was sorry to think he would, yet again, re-live the harrowing details of the car smash that had so destroyed his world.

One might think – and who could blame them? – such sombre beginnings would only depress and mar our part in the celebrations for Alan Brownjohn's 75th birthday. But life, and the life of the emotions, isn't like that. Despite the initial sadness, despite the intense heat, it was a sufficiently memorable event to be worth writing about: something which is seldom true of book launches and the like (despite the fact that, before the advent of e-mail, I used to write many such accounts in letters to daughter Elizabeth in the far flung bits of the globe where she has insisted on residing over the years). Many of the worthies of the English poetry world were at the party, as well as distinguished prose writers (whom I didn't know or recognize) and lifelong friends of Alan Brownjohn: for Alan has always kept himself at 'the centre of things' in the capital.

At our table beside the open window overlooking the traffic-gripped shopping street of Swiss Cottage, apart from Dannie Abse, the small, silver tousle-haired Welsh-Jew, we had Fleur Adcock, in a pale blue dress, very straight-backed, with a gently rictus smile beneath her glittering eyes, signifying a sort of literary contentedness at recently having received the Queen's Gold Medal for Poetry. Only the third woman to do so. Jokingly I asked her to show it me, but her look showed great uncertainty as to how to take my remark, and she said she hadn't got it with her. I didn't tell her that I had seen and handled Kathleen Raine's medal – Kathleen being the first female to get the only 'gong' for poetry other than the Laureateship. Next to Fleur was Elaine Feinstein on her right, and crushed up against her on the other like a fat clown in shorts was Hugging John Horder, spinning I know not what plaints and tales. John is the great apostle of hugging as the cure for all the world's ills, hence his well-earned prefix. On the other side of the table were Patricia, Leah Fritz and myself.

With the advent of food, our little gathering broke up. Floating round the room on Rimbaud's *bateau ivre* I encountered other persons like the ever-friendly Aussie poet Peter Porter still recalling his memorably enjoyable visit to the Torbay Poetry Festival last year ('I even enjoyed my own reading for once!' he had said at the time); plus a woman who said her name was 'Sally' and who, for some reason, chose to discuss the large quantity of red lipstick she uses which, 'Always gets left on my wine glass'. To which I retorted, 'I suppose it's better than on men's shirts?' But I could see she disagreed with that, so I passed on.

Having just had a communication that very morning from Martin Bax, editor of *Ambit,* telling me he wished to use two of my poems, I was pleased to bump into him right in the thick of the party. We talked some while about the two poems he was going to use in the special issue to celebrate 'the 150th anniversary of Freud's birth'. Having once read the sex-doctor's huge tome entitled *The Interpretation of Dreams*, and could quote a line from it, it gave some credence to Martin's belief that my poem 'Beyond The Pleasure Principle' makes me a dyed-in-the-poetics Freudian. When, in reality, I am – and have always been – much more interested in Jung, especially his *Memories, Dreams and Reflections*, which always prevents me from recalling the Freud masterpiece – the title of which I always have to resort to Patricia for. Speaking of whom, in the course of my reception room ramble and *bateau ivre* sailing, I naturally kept re-encountering, along with David Perman, my publisher, and Danielle. The latter having just handed a skinhead partygoer onto me with the words, 'This is John. He wants somebody to argue with about poetry and translation. I thought of you straight away.' Immediately we began to debate this and that, especially the Skinhead's claim that his Romanian girlfriend was 'perfectly bilingual', and that he was her translator looking to get her work published. I said it was impossible to be 'perfectly bilingual – one belongs to one language or another, never can be native to both.' But if his girlfriend was, as he claimed, perfectly bilingual then why did she need a translator? He failed to see the contradiction. At which point Patricia; and a poet whom I dubbed 'Striped Shirt' (keen to tell everyone that he had recently figured on 'the front cover of the magazine *Agenda*'); and 'the perfectly bilingual' and beautiful Romanian named Ariadne, joined us and, somehow, I fell out of the discourse. Patricia took over, ending up at a corner table 'like a sage or queen bee with adoring acolytes', according to David Perman. In her own words, this is the substance of the dialogue that then ensued:

The Skinhead wanted to talk about translations and for a while I just listened politely, adding such wise comments as, 'Oh I think so too' and 'Really?' and listening to the debate between him and Striped Shirt...who told us yet again about his *Agenda* triumph.

'You have to get the ideas and culture over first; it's no good just getting the rhyme and the metre if the ideas and the culture are not represented. Then work on the rhymes etc., if possible, for you know what the English language is like for rhyming ....' I let him talk for a while more; my head happy with the white wine.

'Do you know of a translator called Brockway?' Skinhead didn't, so I told him about the Briton who had been knighted in Holland for translating so much Dutch literature into English. 'Brockway believed you should do both – the ideas *and* the form. A very talented man.' But it seemed talent wasn't what he wanted to talk about, except the 'talent' of Ariadne and the translations they were doing together of a contemporary Romanian poet whose name I didn't get.

'He's brilliant!' exclaimed Skinhead. Striped Shirt began to look bored. 'Wrote during the communist régime and never used coded language.'

'Yes, he did,' contradicted Ariadne, who, being Romanian, would have known. 'Many of his metaphors and images had double meanings.'

'But that's normal in poetry,' began Skinhead ...

'Yes, lots of English poets write with double meanings, especially in the universities...' began Striped Shirt earnestly in his quiet, teacherish, voice. But Skinhead was an enthusiast and could shout down any teacher.

'But he [the Romanian poet] didn't do it for political reasons!'

(Ariadne was certain he did and when asked for examples said she would look them up for him.) 'That's the point about English poets, they don't write about politics. Now look at Byron: his *Don Juan* is wonderful; it's like a soap opera, it's got everything and ...'

'Never got past the first canto myself ...' added Striped Shirt, 'It's just so banal. It's ...' Again he wasn't allowed to finish.

'It's wonderful. Unlike Keats.'

That did it! Keats, the poet I fell in love with at school, falling asleep quoting 'Thou wast not born for death, immortal bird, /No hungry generations tread thee down...' How dare he! .... I called him a very unlady-like name.

'Byron is wonderful, but so is Keats. His five great odes are some of the best things in English Poetry...' I let him have it from the hip; I'd studied Keats in depth for my BA a few years ago and it all rose up, ready and fluent. Thank goodness for that one large glass of Chardonnay....

'Yes, Byron's *Don Juan* is wonderful, but so is Keats' sensuality and questing. And I love Shelley's intellectualism, his broad-minded approach to poetry. You can't dismiss those so glibly,' I ended.

Striped Shirt was smiling and nodding at this point; I was talking down Skinhead from a genuine passionate enthusiasm. No wonder David Perman thought I was acting like a Queen Bee I was and for once in my life, actually enjoying it.

Having made my point this argument began to cool and I was questioned on whether I was a poet or not. On learning I was a magazine editor, Skinhead began to look thoughtful. Striped Shirt knew about *Acumen* (he should do, for though I have published him, I have also turned him down – a thing all poets remember!) and put Skinhead right. Striped Shirt turned to me,

'You get an Arts Council grant for your magazine. What is your target audience?'

I became careful. 'All readers. The general readers. I try to publish the best poetry I can get hold of which is also accessible to an intelligent reader?' Skinhead nodded and added "Yes, that's right. We need that sort of magazine....'

He was interrupted by Striped Shirt. 'But why not 'academic' poetry? Surely you have a duty with an Arts Council grant to publish material from the universities?'

'Why?'

'Because it's where the youth is. It's where they communicate. You should have a website!'

As it happens, I do have a small website which I use to publicize the magazine, put up poems, add other *Acumen*-oriented events etc, etc. But his dogmatic assertion worried me.

'Why?' I countered.

'Because it's the method of communication by youth. They only read the Web. If it's not on the Web it's nothing.'

Skinhead remarked that was probably true, but to have something in lasting form was better. So did Ariadne who thought that poetry couldn't be read like technical information on-screen. I remarked that it probably could but that you couldn't curl up with your computer screen, take it to bed with you, read it in the bath ... Of course, the verbal beginnings of poetry came up, but as we all finally agreed, once printing became available most poets jumped at having their work in the more permanent form.

As a parting shot after much more cut-and-thrust conversation, Skinhead suddenly said, 'If anyone claims it is the poetry that gets lost in translation, just quote the St. James' Version of the *Bible*. Now that brings over ideas, culture and a wonderful language.'

But, interesting as the discussion was, it was time for me to leave the party. Before I departed, however, Striped Shirt offered me his card and told us all yet again he was on the cover of the latest issue of *Agenda* ...

While that Patricia was thus engaged in such stimulating wrangling, I went in search of our host to get him to inscribe the copy of the chunky yellow-and-pink-covered *Collected Poems of Alan Brownjohn,* published by subscription for this very occasion. I eventually found the birthday boy in conversation with his old chum Anthony Thwaite. Alan seemed half-wrapped in a pale flogiston of dream. He said he was tired; but was not too fatigued to wield his pen in fulsome inscription of my copy of the book.

Shortly before we left, Kit Wright – who is the tallest poet in the British Isles at about seven feet – arrived. He said he was late because he had been with his first wife who is dying. The abiding image I have closing this evening was that of most people having left, and Patricia and I and David and Danielle about to depart. Kit Wright was looking down on both myself and Anthony Thwaite, and Patricia and others maybe. Thwaite, who is a small man, was craning his neck backwards to see up the Wright Mountain, and Kit was saying directly to me, 'It's odd how one's ex-wives always seem to get on so well? You wouldn't think it would be so.' A remark that brought back memories of how my Austrian friend Wolfgang's first and second wives used to play tennis together and go to keep-fit classes, 'In order that they could share perceptions of the male shortcomings.' A sentiment that the Tall Poet would no doubt have agreed with.

24.
THE LIVING DEAD

We travelled up from Cheltenham for John Heath-Stubbs' funeral, little realizing I was living into my anecdotage once more. Because it was winter, and because there had been flooding in the Severn Tunnel, and because we had to change to a train from Cardiff to Paddington at Bristol Parkway, Patricia and I just beat the coffin into the church of St. Matthew's, Bayswater. A congregation of about a hundred people was already present filling the central pews either side the main aisle, so we went and parked ourselves among the deserted side pews, but in a position from where we could see the proceedings clearly. The church had a rather shabby air to it, but it was to provide a generous, even happy service of which I felt John would have approved.

As the coffin came slowly into the church accompanied by John's most actively caring friend Guthrie McKie, and by Eddie Linden, his other great helper, I glanced back, partly to see the entry of the coffin, and partly to see if I could recognize anyone. Three pew rows back on my right my gaze briefly met that of Oliver Bernard, brother of the late and more famous Jeffrey Bernard who used to sit in the Coach & Horses in Soho publicly drinking himself to death and writing a weekly column about the experience in *The Spectator.* When Jeffrey had died a play entitled *Jeffrey Bernard Is Unwell* was staged in the West End. As for Oliver, a poet best known for his translations of Rimbaud, I had briefly known him as a fellow member of the infamous General Council of the Poetry Society in the troubled early 'Nineties. Beyond seeing him as the coffin came in I recognized nobody else, save for Guthrie McKie.

Looking back with hindsight it may have been my imagination but I thought Oliver Bernard looked a bit startled when we spotted each other. The service soon put all other thoughts out of my head however. After an unpromising beginning in which the somewhat bumbling, hirsute vicar began a mumbled speech away from the pulpit microphone so that few people could hear him, until some despairing member of the congregation pointed the fact out, Sebastian Barker read an extract from St. Paul which must have had some relevance to or for the departed, but which I failed to pick up on. However, Sebastian at least was perfectly audible. There then followed an excellent, lengthy and well-rounded, peroration about the life of Heath-Stubbs from his old tutor and friend Professor John Jones of Merton College Oxford. The final speech came from Guthrie, and it was mainly concerned with thanking the nurses and other carers who had made John's last months bearable. It was also interesting to learn that Guthrie's friendship was not a literary one but simply that of a close neighbour of the departed in Notting Hill. These addresses to the congregation were, of course, interspersed with hymn singing and prayers.

The service over – and the coffin taken away for interment at Kensal Green Cemetery – there followed a wake at the rear end of the church: and a wake such as John would have heartily approved having, in his lifetime, become somewhat of an expert in such occasions. As, of course, is the wont of these functions at the start there develops immediately the poetry world's equivalent of a rugby scrum in front of the bar – or if it is a long bar there will be several such tussles – eventually though everyone manages to get his or her free drink. But, as the drink is 'on the house' or, on this occasion, 'on the church', much is consumed and there is a constant toing-and-froing to the bar.

Having obtained my first glass of what turned out to be a rather good *Côte de Quelque Chose*, I had just turned away from the trestle table that made do for a bar, when I ran into one Paul Birtill, a stocky figure of a man who happens to write poems and plays. In his poetry Paul is notoriously pessimistic, often suggesting the best way to live life is not to. Anyway, on his round, pale visage – a genial visage despite his aforementioned outlook on life – on his face was an expression wildly circulating made up of such elements as surprise, amazement, shock and disbelief. Liking Paul, I naturally greeted him in a friendly way but which he quite ignored saying in a slightly hoarse voice, 'But...but I was told you were dead!'

Now I expect we all have our different ways of responding to such information. But, in my case, it was a literary, indeed a poetic, way I coped with it. I remained silent pondering deeply not so much what Paul Birtill had said, as thinking I may well have been, at that moment, the first English poet since Robert Graves to hear of his own death. He was reported killed in action in the First World War, and had come out of a coma in the field hospital to read a copy of his own obituary in *The Times*. Being vocally informed of my own demise, I felt quite proudly, was the next best thing to reading of it. When I finally surfaced from this reverie, Paul had drifted away, probably embarrassed at having so stunned me.

Next, having gulped down my wine, I immediately rejoined the fray to obtain a second glass, which I eventually obtained. Once again, turning from the bar I found myself confronted by Dinah Livingstone, poet, editor and publisher. Said she to me, 'I was sorry to hear you'd been so ill. But you look fine now.'

'Er, yes, I feel fine. But I should tell you, Dinah, I haven't been ill.'

'Oh, I thought you had. I must have been thinking of someone else.'

Nevertheless, I could not resist telling her what Birtill had said to me; and how pleased I was to think I might be the first poet since Graves to hear of his own demise. Deep down I suspect that poets are secretly pleased to feel they have some input into what F.R. Leavis called 'the Great Tradition'; or, in this case, the even more exclusive tradition of poets hearing of their own death. And when, finally, I had bored Dinah with my expatiating on the poetic and symbolic implications of what had come to pass, we drifted off in different directions: in this religious place seeking pastures new or, at any rate, further topping up of our glasses. But, almost immediately, I ran into Patricia and she said, 'Guess what Leah Fritz has just said to me?' 'What?' I queried. 'She said she was sorry to hear you had been very ill, but you looked alright now.'

Reeling slightly from this repetitive misinformation I, of course, informed my wife of all that I had just told Dinah Livingstone. While, I was telling her this, someone else of our acquaintance, but whose name escapes me now – Anne-Marie Fyfe perhaps? – passed by and said she was glad to see how well I was looking. 'I wonder who is spreading this story, these stories...?' Patricia said. I mentioned Birtill and said I would go and find out who had told him the grim news about me. 'Yes, do that, and let me know when you find out.' Patricia.

So, after procuring myself yet another drink, I proceeded to search for Birtill. In the process I got waylaid talking with Kit Wright, a wonderful guy but one whom a conversation with is like permanently craning one's neck at a cloud, on account of his exceptional tallness and magnificent head of white hair. Eventually, though, I did find Birtill and I demanded to know where he had got the idea I had already departed to that Temple of Very Little Fame on Mount Parnassus, and was startled by his answer. 'It was Oliver Bernard who told me.'

At this piece of information I immediately thought, well, yes, this is possible given the Bernard family's evident preoccupation with public dyings. Either it was that, or wishful thinking on the part of someone who had imparted the misinformation to Oliver. As soon as Birtill named the possible culprit, I set off to search for Oliver. But try as I might, and question as many people as possible, getting the frequent answer 'Oh, yes, Oliver's here...well he was?', he was, in fact, nowhere to be found. Maybe the sight of me at the beginning of the church service had totally unnerved him and he had fled? Possibly, he may have had more pressing business that had forced him to cut the wake. But, as Oliver is a poet, and poets are the very staunchest supporters of wakes, book launches...and weddings of the sort they had at Canna, it was unlikely that he had left of his own free will.

All I could, in the end, think of was that this event proved I was now truly in my anecdotage, as fate or something was writing my reminiscences for me.

25.
FALLING ASLEEP IN THE PALACE

It would be fair to describe Patricia as a Renaissance Woman. An excellent cook and gardener on the domestic front and, away from that front, a skilled organizer of events such as an annual poetry festival together with other poetry events between times. Additionally, she has run a high quality literary journal devoted to poetry for over thirty years. And the more she became involved in the world of poetry she decided to seek a second academic qualification different from her scientific training in analytical chemistry, with the result she went to a London university and attained a first class honour's degree in English Literature.

A consequence of the work (or should one say works?) that Patricia had undertaken over the years, it was inevitable that someone would feel that her efforts should be publically honoured. The main mover in this effort to bring governmental, and then royal attention to Patricia was a close friend of ours ,whom royal etiquette requires to be nameless. And so it came to pass in 2011 that Patricia was summoned to Buckingham Palace to be awarded an MBE for 'Services to poetry',

I have always been delighted by my wife's every achievement. It has been a perfect satisfaction to me each time she achieved something as a result of her efforts. Over the years I wrote my poems and, from time to time, had them published. While Patricia, who pens the occasional prose essay or book review, puts most of her efforts into organizing things, as indicated; and this brief chapter tells the story of the day we and our two daughters, Kate and Elizabeth, went to the Palace for the awards' ceremony.

For me the grandeur of the occasion was quite exceeded by the incredible efficiency of the ceremony. Asked to be present well before the 11am start, we arrived in a car which Elizabeth had arranged to take us from the small, unprepossessing hotel run by a very pleasant Indian family. We were escorted through the main entrance to Buckingham Palace by an equerry or two: perfectly charming, ex-military men I suspect. The first thing they asked of us was to give up our mobile phones, and I was assigned the task of taking them, together with our coats, to a cloakroom. Next, the ladies required to repair to what, in the circumstances, might be called 'the Royal Flush' to powder their noses, etc. Then we were ushered, along with many other visitors, up a grand flight of stairs, and Elizabeth, Kate and myself were directed one way off the stairs and Patricia in another direction. We entered a vast ballroom with a small dais at one end and many rows of seats facing it.

At some point, the three of us were given a sort of Order of Service booklet which listed all those to be honoured in the hour and a quarter allotted to the event. The people to receive an award were drawn from different spheres of work: industry, armed forces, the arts, sport and so forth. Unfortunately, reading through the booklet I saw a name I thought I recognized, namely one Colin Firth. 'Isn't he a footballer?' I queried. My daughters were horrified at my ignorance and hissed simultaneously that he was an actor. The number of persons to be honoured was 107, and I could not believe they would be all fitted into a mere hour and a quarter. But such was the impressive efficiency of the whole ceremony they were. And Prince Charles still managed to have a few friendly words with each of the persons honoured: a charming engagement by His Highness, whether he was handing out a knighthood or an MBE. I confess I do not expect to see such a leisurely-seeming super efficiency anywhere else in society, unless it be at a military parade.

After the glittering ceremony was over, all trouped down the grand stairs and out into a courtyard for photographs. It was a bit like the aftermath of a wedding in that respect. Some of those present being well-known public figures, one of whom was the footballer, sorry, actor Colin Firth who had played Mr D'Arcy on TV in Jane Austin's *Pride and Prejudice*. Patricia, having been greatly taken by the actor's performance would have liked to have met him, but was not self-confident enough to go up and introduce herself. However, daughter Elizabeth suffering no such inhibitions went straight over to him and said her mother was a fan of his and would like to meet him. He proved perfectly amenable to this, and to being photographed with her as well, and the pleasure of the encounter was subsequently almost more discussed than the award of the MBE.

A friend of Elizabeth and Barry's, Sheila O'Conner, a few months earlier had also been awarded an MBE, so we had known something of the proceedings in advance. Sheila who, like Barry, works for the

Foreign Office, and is the person responsible for things like organizing Royal visits when foreign heads of state are scheduled to meet the Queen. Today, Sheila was assigned responsibility for greeting and looking after the guests at the post-award dinner which Patricia was to give at Carluccio's Italian restaurant in the Covent Garden.

When we Palace-guests arrived at the restaurant, we were welcomed by Sheila and three of our grandchildren, namely, Iain, Emma and Katy-Rose. In addition, the guest list consisted of literary friends, like William and Wendy Marshall, Dannie Abse, Lynne Hjelmgaard, Leah and Howard Fritz, Glyn and Parvin Pursglove, David Perman and Danielle Hope and others like and Fran and Tony Morris, Elizabeth and Kate. Unfortunately, John and Gina Wilson couldn't attend as John was recovering from an operation. The particular restaurant had been chosen because it was situated opposite the Garrick Club of which Roy Davids was a member. He had invited us all for post-prandial champagne; however this part of the long luncheon did not materialize because Roy became dizzy on entering the Garrick Club and left town to go and see his doctor. But everything else went splendidly and all Patricia's guests gave every appearance of hugely enjoying themselves sharing in the honour of the occasion. And the three grandchildren, under the directorship of Iain, performed a specially-written play for Patricia MBE.

The grandchildren, ah, yes, they are alert to everything. One of the features of an award ceremony at Buckingham Palace is that each individual award is filmed on CD which can be bought. Patricia's was purchased and, apart from concentrating on her entering the grand ballroom, wearing a brand new dress and tottering on high heels, and having Price Charles pin the MBE on her chest, the film-maker panned his camera around the audience, pausing for a second at each small group of friends or relatives. As luck would have it, I blinked the moment the camera caught me and, of course, when the CD came to us a few days later, it showed me with my eyes shut. It was with the greatest glee the three grandchildren accused me of having 'fallen asleep in the Palace'…making it, of course, sound like high treason.

26.
PICKING UP THE PIECES

2014 was a difficult year for Patricia and myself. It got off to a bad start in December 2013 with the ending of the twenty five year marriage of Kate, our younger daughter.

Patricia's birthday is 3rd February and it is the custom to celebrate it each year with John and Gina Wilson, our friends from Cheltenham – who also have a flat in Torquay. Anyway, we were dining with them and the maritally-emancipated daughter Kate, when a 'phone call came through at the very start of the meal, which Patricia did not answer straight away but let it record on the answering machine. Later, after the meal was over and the Wilsons had left she listened to the message. It was from Hilary Davies to tell us her husband, the poet, Sebastian Barker was dead. We went up to London to attend the funeral on the 19th February at St. Ignatius'Church in Stamford Hill where, incidentally, nearly twenty years' before we had attended Sebastian and Hilary's wedding.

Sebastian, Patricia and I were friends for many years, and his death was a particular blow to us: adding a further potion to an already difficult mixture this year.

The funeral itself was just as Sebastian would have wanted it, I know. Patricia, myself and Danielle Hope met up with David Perman at the Church and, at the appropriate time, a full requiem mass followed. As with all Roman Catholic churches, St. Ignatius's was a panoply of gilded imagery: bright décor and much to please the eye, lift the spirits. Many well-known poetry literati were there, of course, and many others.

After the service was over, there was to be a private interment in the City of London cemetery, followed by a wake at two thirty in the afternoon in Stoke Newington town hall. This created an interlude of two and a half hours in the proceedings. So Alan Brownjohn, Peter and Diana Carter, Nancy Mattson and Michael Bartholomew-Biggs, Dinah Livingstone, David Perman, the sculptor Paul Kincaid and girlfriend, plus ourselves, decided to go off as a group and find somewhere to have lunch.

A short bus ride was called for, as David insisted we go to nearby Stoke Newington to eat. This was sensible enough, in that we had to go later on to the town hall there for the wake for Sebastian. David said, as the required bus approached, 'I'll tell you where to get off!' At this my stomach tightened for a minute or two, for I knew that any group of poets can hardly ever agree on anything, even where to alight from transport. By the time the second bus-stop approached, Mike and Nancy insisted it was the place to get off and promptly pressed the stop bell. They – plus, for some reason Paul Kincaid and his girlfriend whom Nancy and Mike had only just met – followed the latter's instant leadership and alighted. While the rest of us stayed loyal to General Perman – despite some doubtful murmurings. Hearing which mutterings of mutiny, David said sharply he knew Stoke Newington well, as one of his daughters lived there. As a consequence we, the Perman faction, alighted at the far end of Stoke Newington High Street. Whereas more sensibly, as it turned out, the Bartholomew-Biggs rebels had alighted at the start of the said street where the restaurants began.

When our group got off the bus, it was approximately opposite a pub on the other side of the street called The Daniel Defoe, after the author of many works, most famously *Robinson Crusoe*. This seemed a good omen, and Peter Carter said, in his rich South African voice: 'I need a drink!' So I suggested we cross the street to this literary pub. But Alan Brownjohn sprang to life with the almost-shouted words: 'Oh, I know a marvellous pub just a bit further up this street!' And despite being eighty years of age, he bounded off up the street, leaving us no option but to follow him. (It's amazing how easy it is for any of us to become dictators!) Soon we were in sight of Stoke Newington town hall itself when Alan, risking life and limb as they say, swerved across the street to an establishment that looked more like an animal pet shop than a pub. Scarcely had Alan reached it, than he turned round and indicated to us not to cross over. When he re-joined us, with puzzled demeanour, he said: 'It's shut…I can't understand it as it's the lunch hour now.' But, as always, David came to the rescue with the words: 'Don't worry, I know another excellent pub…just wait here.' With which he shot across the street, leaving the rest of us talking on the pavement. Actually, I delivering a mini-monologue on Defoe above Carter's occasional refrain of 'I need a drink!' David re-emerged from the narrow entry across the street down which he had temporarily disappeared. He, too, retraced his footsteps back across the street reciting à la

Brownjohn: 'It's shut…I can't understand it as it's the lunch hour now.' Adding, 'You'd think pubs would be open at this time.'

Somewhat forlornly we began a procession back along the street, with Peter reiterating in his rich South African accent, 'I need a drink!' about every thirty paces or so – the matter was becoming serious as most of us shared his view. Abruptly, once more David crossed the street as we drew level again with The Daniel Defoe. But it, too, proved to be shut. So, finally, we were forced to begin an examination of the cafes and restaurants. Almost the first we encountered was an unprepossessing café with huge windows from which, looking smugly at us, was Mike and Nancy's group. This occasioned yet another debate as to whether we should suffer loss of face and go in and join them. It didn't appear the sort of place that served alcohol and, with Carter continuing to bellow his need, our hesitancy grew. The consensus finally was that we should continue our search for a pub. But, then, two things happened. Dinah Livingstone deserted our group with the words: 'Well, I'm going in – I'm fed up of wandering up and down this bloody street!' And Peter exclaimed, 'Ah, man, there's an off-licence! You guys go in the café and I'll get us some drinks. I'll pay whatever corking charge they charge.' And he disappeared into the off-licence nearby.

Meanwhile, into the café the rest of us went and re-joined the others. Once inside, David Perman made an unexpected announcement to the café's lady proprietor. He said: 'I'm Danielle Hope's partner, and you may recall some years ago you made a birthday cake at Danielle's behest? Well, it was for this lady's birthday.' (Indicating Patricia.) So it was smiles all round. Then Carter strode in to the accompaniment of the clinking of bottles of wine. Said he to the woman proprietor: 'I'll pay any corking charge.' To which the lady replied: 'We sell wines, beers…even spirits with our meals.' But not to be outdone and, for another saving of face, Carter gestured magisterially: 'Good lady, have the wine and distribute it to all of my friends here…and if we run out, I'll buy from you.'

Not to prolong this digression too much, I'll just say that we all had a good meal: the highpoint of which for me was not the food, but my publisher Perman produced three copies of my, as yet unpublished, *Collected and New Poems*. Then at almost 2.30pm. we all traipsed off to the nearby town hall for Sebastian Barker's wake. This took place in a giant, high-ceilinged, ballroom-sized room – with a long bar set against one wall, and a dozen tables on the other side of the room. Here we met Sebastian's daughters Miranda and Xanthe, and his previous wife – the one immediately before Hilary snared him into the arms of herself and the Roman Catholic church. Amongst the poetry *afficianados* I encountered, in addition to Hilary, were Shaun Traynor; Michael Mackmin editor of *The Rialto* who has never liked my poetry; James Harpur, editor of *Temenos Academy Journal,* who does like my poetry; Michael Glover, who has probably never read any of my poetry – his real interest being painting.

Last word on Sebastian's funeral and wake – a better (if that's the right word?) occasion than even that of John Heath-Stubbs's seven years previously: at which, as I recorded, Sebastian had read an epistle of St. Paul. – But back now to where this digression began: to the matter of change and removals.

*   *   *   *   *

The day the publisher of my *Collected and New Poems* left Brixham (having brought me more copies of the book) to return to the Home Counties, Alan Murray and Alison Varndel arrived – a young couple with a poetic side to them and, in Alison's case, a passionate love of animals, especially cats, dogs and birds. In the five days in March they were with us, there was a Poet's Friday event, run by Patricia and the print-maker Deborah Treliving, at Cockington Court, Torquay; and on Sunday, 16th March, a Poetry Day organized by Patricia in the Brixham Theatre function room. And, though we knew it was in the wind, yet another removal was about to take place: this time of my literary archive of letters, book-proofs, notebooks, etc., which the British Library wished to acquire.

First, though, the archive had to be brought down from our loft and got ready for John Wilson, in his capacity of manuscript dealer, to collect and transport to Cheltenham where it would be examined by a representative of the British Library's contemporary poetry archivist. It was fortunate that Alan and Alison were staying with us, as Alan greatly assisted in the bringing down of the archive into our conservatory. Equally fortunate was the presence of Tony Morris when, on the following Sunday Poetry Day, in the absence of Alan, Alison and Patricia, he was able to help with the loading up of John's vehicle with the archive to take to Cheltenham. So, as I say, though this further 'removal' was not unexpected, we had only a few days' notice of the actual date of the collection.

After this there were, of course, a number of less demanding occasions. Like a pleasant visit to Devon poetry publisher Alwyn Marriage who, with her husband Hugh, sailed us up the River Avon in their boat from South Pool to North Shore, Salcombe, to give us lunch. But none especially demanding until the 2nd May.

For some time Danielle Hope, Patricia's advisory editor on *Acumen,* had been talking about reviving the annual Acumen party which had fallen into desuetude because her house was no longer large enough to host the numbers likely to attend. But as a professor now at King's College in London, Danielle was able to arrange for the revived party to take place at the university's premises in the Strand. Also, she combined the event with the launch of my *Collected and New Poems* from Rockingham Press.

It had taken about three years to edit this 'volume of a lifetime' of poems by which 'one would like to be remembered'...to employ various traditional phrases used about such a volume. Because I had written so many poems over the years – and had had a *Collected Longer Poems* twenty years earlier – I asked Patricia and Danielle to assist me in getting the collection down to manageable size; and I knew that always the publisher, would provide sensible critical input as well.

All went well with the final selection; all went well with the production – David Perman producing a beautiful book with a cover designed by Emma Carter (to whom we took a copy soon after the delivery of a boxful in mid-March: she and her husband Dave thoroughly approving of it). Unfortunately, sometime around the end of March, beginning of April, I was dreadfully upset to discover a flaw in the volume, and it was this: no acknowledgement had been made of those journals and magazines – and not a few either – that had published some of the new and hitherto uncollected poems. I took the oversight excessively to heart, considering it entirely my fault. It may have come about subconsciously because I always remember what Robert Graves said about his collected poems: something about poems being 'their own recommendation' and not needing any egotistical listing of which editors had approved of them by earlier publication in their magazines.

Anyway, though, the omission was mine – given the fact that endorsements, acknowledgements, are so much more insisted on now than in Graves's day – I felt the volume doomed to go critically unnoticed by reviewers. So this error, quite frankly, led to a touch of depression – not a thing I normally suffer from. And, in turn, this led to a paranoia about the launch at King's College; and, indeed that, plus the fact that Patricia and I were going to Murcia in Spain early the next day where Iain was studying for his Spanish exams, made me dread both the launch and the visit to Spain. Further factors helped my paranoia, too, like the fact that no member of our family came to the launch, despite having received invitations. Even Iain's sister Emma, who lived in digs in the Borough couldn't find time to attend. Looking back, of course, I realise that the launch was at the May bank holiday when many people go away.

However, the outcome of the not-happily anticipated two events – the party at King's College and the holiday in Spain – was quite different. It was the best party and most glittering event *Acumen* has ever had (with the single exception of the launch at Bonhams' auction house of the Acumen Publications' *First Sixty* anthology); *and* I actually enjoyed the reading I gave from my *Collected and New Poems*. Equally, others must have enjoyed it, too, as 27 copies were sold which I was asked to personally inscribe.

Early next morning, in a better frame of mind, Patricia and I caught a train from St. Pancras Station to Gatwick and flew to Alicante where Iain met us. And just over an hour from Alicante we arrived in Murcia: a small, beautiful, non-touristy city that Elizabeth later described aptly as 'like a little Rome'.

But not here will I recount in detail our stay there, other than to acknowledge the three of us – one student and two old fogeys – had a fine time. Some other time and somewhere else I may write of this holiday: though Patricia and I did compose a 'guest blog' for Iain, giving our doings of the Spanish week, and our impressions of the place.

Between our return home from Spain and a further visit to Cheltenham, then London again, we attended the launch of poet Lynne Wycherley's new book of poems in Exeter on 17th May; and Elizabeth and Barry came down to Brixham from London for a week to continue getting their new house in fully habitable order.

The reason for our visit to Cheltenham was because a minor snag had arisen over the transfer of my archive to the British Library. This was simply that the library did not want thirty odd years of Christmas, birthday, sympathy and other greetings' cards that were scattered among the boxes of letters – even though the majority of such cards were from fellow poets and literary figures. Consequently, Patricia and I had to go to John and Gina's house – where the archive still was – and extract the large quantity of such cards. This we achieved in approximately twenty four hours before leaving first for the British Library where we met the two archivists who wanted the collection; then going on to Enfield for the launch of *Acumen* 79 and a reading by me from my new collection. At Enfield we spent a splendidly hosted day with Alan and Alison, followed by the evening event at which Judi Benson, Wynne Wheldon and Dinah Livingstone read with me. According to Alan it was the largest audience the Enfield Poets' group had had to date.

Next day we spent mostly with Danielle, and we ended it with a visit to the eternal-immortal Torriano for a poetry reading by Leah Fritz and Alan Brownjohn. Then home to Brixham on 9th June.

Reverting a moment to daughter Kate's marital break-up, where this chapter of memoir began. Given that I had not 'seen it coming', Patricia and Elizabeth, our other daughter, had expressed the view that I had virtually no powers of perception in matters of the heart. At least, unlike them, had not seen in Kate's case 'trouble brewing'. However, something awaited us when we got back home from London that seemed to give the lie to that. Let me explain.

At the previous Christmas, our friends Emma and Dave Carter (as I said, Emma designed the cover of my new Collected Poems) had brought a framed photograph of Patricia and myself at a fancy dress occasion at Agatha Christie's Greenway House as a present. They didn't stay long as they were out delivering presents to various other friends. Patricia and I expressed our pleasure at what they had brought, and only regretted that we had not thought of a present for them. But promised them an inscribed copy of my Collected Poems later in the New Year.

Then three things happened. First, while we were away in Spain, the framed photographic Christmas gift fell off our front room wall and broke. Then, some three weeks later Patricia sent a notice out reminding people of the 15th June launch of my new book in Brixham. By return e-mail she received an apology from Emma Carter saying because of 'a big family commitment' she wouldn't be able to attend the launch of the book. When I had absorbed this rather enigmatic message, I exclaimed: 'I don't like this – it's like that cup of your mother's that just fell to pieces a few days before she died. Then the broken picture. Now this odd turn-down over the book launch. It must mean something…Maybe she and Dave are parting company like Kate and her husband?'

As I have said, I was experiencing a touch of paranoia at this time; and Patricia knew this. Naturally, she dismissed what I said about Emma and Dave as absurd. Then, the day after we got back from London on 9th June, Patricia received this email, in answer to an enquiry of hers as to the location of Emma's upcoming summer painting exhibition:

'It's in Loddiswell, but why not wait until August when you can see the big island artist show? Things have changed between Dave and myself and, unfortunately, we are now separated and getting a divorce. It will be a shock I'm sure and upsetting, but it's a long story and one I never wanted to tell… – Emma.'

All that Patricia could find to say on receipt of that email was, 'I really do believe now that pigs can fly!' We both did in fact. And thought, well, it just had to be the last act of loss in this year of losses. But not so.

Then came this: Dannie Abse died on 28th September.

Patricia was so moved by the death of our friend that she composed a warm personal memoir of Dannie. This was published in *Acumen* 81 in January 2015. As he was such a good friend to both of us, and as Patricia and I have worked closely together over all the years of the magazine's life, I feel it appropriate to reproduce her memoir:

DANNIE ABSE

I first met Dannie Abse in 1982 at the pizza place in Mortimer Street, gatecrashing somewhat on a lunch-time meeting between him and William. We'd just come back from our first visit to Salzburg and

I was buzzing with the excitement I'd found at the University there. I found him a kind man, generous with the way he involved me in the conversation (I was very shy in those days). This was the first of many meetings over pizzas and I began to look forward to them. I enjoyed listening to his lilting voice, not overtly Welsh but with a cadence of song about it. I was drawn to his anecdotes about poets whom – at that time – I'd only heard of, never met. I loved his spontaneous laughter and sense of humour; his mild ribbing of poets and poetry. I was absorbed into the seriousness of his poetics and his writing. This is not to say of course, that the pizzas were not eaten without incidents – with both Dannie and William present, they couldn't be. There was the time, deep in conversation, that William mistook the waiter who asked politely if he wanted his pizza hot. "Of course," replied William wondering why anyone would want to eat cold pizza. His first mouthful caused his face to go red, his eyes to water and produced a bout of coughing which shook the restaurant. And Dannie, who tried to be so sympathetic between gusts of laughter and pouring out lashings of water!

Another time, Dannie had gone in first to the restaurant and William had stopped to hang up his coat. As we passed a table, someone whom we knew slightly jumped up and demanded to know if that had been Dannie Abse who had preceded us and on being reassured it was, immediately tagged along saying, "You must introduce me, you must introduce me!" Luckily Dannie had procured a table for three so the introduction did not lead to an interloper during the meal. It was at one of the tables there in the summer of 1984 that William suddenly said to Dannie: "Patricia's going to start a literary magazine." Dannie immediately put his hand into his pocket, pulled out a fiver and slapped it on the table. "Put me down as a subscriber," he insisted. Then, the serious business of pizzas over, he remarked, "You'll need some contributions. I've nearly finished at the clinic. Give me five minutes and I'll pick you up at the entrance (to the hospital where he worked) and we'll drive to Golders Green and look at what I have. You haven't met Joan yet, have you?"

And that is precisely what happened, I met Joan. Joan, whom I immediately liked and grew to love dearly as I got to know her better. Just a little older than myself, yet infinitely more worldly wise, more prescient, she became a role model for me in how to … well live life!

Dannie and Joan taught me so much …

But back to the contributions. Dannie gave me both prose and poetry contributions for the first issue and continued right up to his death to send me work. It was at another meal in Mortimer Street that William informed him I was going back to university to do a mature student's degree in English. "That's the trouble, with women," said Dannie with mock sorrow, "They show us men up all the time. Take Joan for instance. She went back to university and did History of Art. Wrote a book on Ruskin as well. She has his portrait on her study wall… He's my rival, you know, I think she thinks more of him than of me." And later, "You'll want somewhere to stay while you look for student digs. We'll be away for that week. Come and stay at Hodford Road and look after the cat." And so we met Caitlin, a beautiful and aristocratic female ginger and white cat who lorded it over the house. A further chapter had begun.

We stayed on and off at Hodford Road over the following four years, not just when we were looking for digs for we soon became settled, but when Dannie and Joan went away to give readings in many countries from America in the West, to Israel in the East. In fact, we stayed so often during one particular term that a postcard came to the house addressed to "Patricia and William, and Dannie and Joan if they still live there." It was during these years that Dannie retired and his poetry writing began to increase. We would often go for supper and Dannie would read out a new poem, asking us how it sounded. Being immersed in poetry all day (many students managed to avoid reading any poetry while at college; I managed to avoid reading any novels, at least for exam purposes) I was happy to talk about his poetry, occasionally interpreting his writing as I felt there was a depth to a particular poem which wasn't at first obvious. I would argue with Joan and William about the "meaning" while Dannie gave much laughter at our disagreements.

Dannie and William were both involved with the Poetry Society during my stint at Westfield College (alas, now no more, having been amalgamated with Queen Mary's College in the East End, first as QMW then dropping the reference to Westfields and reverting to Queen Mary's), Dannie as President and William on the General Council. To settle debts, it was decided that the premises in Earls Court Square were to be sold and a smaller but more fit-for- purpose (to use a modern cliché) place would be bought in central London. Both have covered the period well in their respective autobiographies so I won't go into it here, but it was chastening to feel that they both tried to put poetry first in what was becoming a bitter battle over property, money and ideology. It was not unexpected that they both resigned before the matter was dealt with finally. Whether the new Betterton Street address was a more fit-for purpose building I leave those who know the place to decide for themselves.

It was during the 1990s that Dannie almost came to Torbay on more than one sporting occasion. Dannie was life-long supporter of Cardiff City Football Club. At that time they played in Division Three (or whatever it was called) and so did Torquay United. But every time Cardiff played in Torquay, Dannie was unfortunately away reading somewhere and he never made it. Then at the end of the season, the teams drifted apart. Cardiff began its rise through the league tables until it reached the championship division; Torquay stayed down, went up for one season but couldn't sustain it, then finally dropped back to the Conference League where they are at the moment. Dannie often commiserated with me about their lack of progress, trying to change my (non)allegiance to cheer for Cardiff City.

However, in the Year of the Artist when the Arts Council decided they wanted a thousand artists of all kinds "in place" for the Millennium Year, Torbay did better than in football. Through a mixture of official arts' tactics and subtle "blackmail" William became Poet-in- Residence for Torbay, tasked with putting poetry into people's lives. He decided to organise a poetry event each month culminating in a short three day Festival in May 2001. At one of these evenings, Dannie and Joan finally travelled to Torquay to repeat one of their "Voices in the Gallery" events at Torre Abbey. It was a wonderful evening, Joan and Dannie reading poems about paintings while showing the painting on a screen – courtesy of power-point. After the interval Dannie gave a reading and the audience of Torbay, relatively new to modern poetry, went away happy and excited and looking forward to further such events. After it finished we took Dannie and Joan for a meal to … where else but a Pizza Express? We showed them a little of Brixham the following morning, confirming Dannie's saying that Heaven rhymes with Devon! They wrote in our visitor's book: "it's been wonderful to visit you and find you bringing a poetry revolution to Torbay." Alas, it was to be some years before Dannie visited Torbay again, and by then, sadly he was alone. Due to open William's mini-Festival in May 2001, Dannie suffered a heart attack and couldn't make it. Though we continued to see him in London, Caitlin had died and we no longer cat sat for the Abses. Also the Torbay Festival and the increasing work-load of the newly-designed *Acumen* magazine meant staying in Brixham for longer periods.

Eventually, having recoverd, Dannie agreed to come and read at the Festival in October 2005. (I had taken over the running of the Festival after the first one.) But again, Dannie didn't make it as that year Joan was killed in a car crash and he cancelled all his reading engagements. Though we continued to visit him at Hodford Road, and though on the surface, he seemed the same Dannie, he wasn't. His laughter had dimmed and his voice had a sadness which never really left it. It wasn't until 2008 that we managed to persuade him to read at the Festival again. A huge success, we had one of our best audiences to date for his reading. And going home on the same train he met Lynne, a beautiful, gentle young widow who was also grieving for a lost beloved husband. Their shared grief, support and affection for each other lasted until Dannie's death. He returned to Torbay once more in 2011 when Lynne was reading at the Festival and took part in a talk about his work and poetry. But after that, he found travelling to give poetry readings tiring (he was approaching ninety years of age) and so we travelled to London to see performances of his plays, to listen to him read, to celebrate fifty years of publishing with Hutchinsons, to celebrate his 90th birthday at a Pizza Express in Hampstead, etc. We continued to have suppers or lunches with him in Golders Green, though sadly his favourite Pizza Express in Golders Green had closed down, and we had to go elsewhere for his second favourite meal of salt beef sandwiches. We still talked poetry, read poems to each other, but it became obvious that though he appeared as sprightly as ever, his laugh still as spontaneous as ever, age was slowing him down.

Earlier this year, my advisory editor, Danielle Hope, resurrected the annual Acumen Party but at Kings College in the Strand, and not at her house in Islington. It was an event combined with the launch of

William's *Collected and New Poems*. Dannie was with us for the whole evening and full of life, surrounded by many of his friends. In September of 2014 I rang him to ask if we could meet while we were in London. It was Lynne who answered the phone and told us Dannie was seriously ill. We managed two further conversations with him over the phone. He talked of his long association with *Acumen* and said 'We made a good team didn't we?' – Good job he couldn't see the tears at my end of the phone.

When I think of Dannie now, what comes into my mind? First and foremost, of course it is poetry; he has left us so much to remember him by. But I think of pizzas and salt beef; Cardiff City; his cry of "Joan, Joan!" whenever he needed help with a decision. And I can't boil potatoes now without remembering how proud Dannie was when, after Joan's death, his daughter had taught him to make mash, and then his sudden switch of mood as, turning to William, he added, "Get Patricia to teach you to cook, that's been one of the hardest things I've had to learn." I miss his laughter, his generosity, his wisdom. He has enriched our life, so much and that of many others. Thank You, Dannie.

*　*　*　*　*

What comes back to me about Dannie are the many small, 'unofficial' details that stacked up to project his warm humanity. How he would always appear for breakfast at the white table in the kitchen at Hodford Road where we mostly ate. Appear just before 8am. in his crumpled pyjamas, his hair tousled grey, his face unshaven. Over breakfast, we would discuss many, often 'learned' things. Like Sebastian Barker, Dannie was always fully awake at breakfast. Then, breakfast over, he would go and bathe or shower and shave. And afterwards, we four, Dannie, Joan, Patricia and me, would go about our separate businesses to write poems, attend lectures in Patricia's case, or write an article on art: Joan being the art critic and historian — hers a serious mind conjoined to a naturally happy visage.

In the late 'Seventies in Theberton Square, Islington, there was a second-hand bookshop that hosted poetry evenings on a regular basis. I used to go there with my former City chum Quentin Lane whenever I was up in London. One of the poetry readings we attended was given by Dannie Abse, and that's how he and I first met. After the reading by the evening's guest poet was over, much of the audience would repair to the Irish Bar next to the bookshop. It was in that pleasant environment that Quentin, myself and another, got talking with Dannie. The other party was an odd man: a happy, smiling Hindi from Calcutta who, strangely, was totally devoted to the work of Samuel Beckett, the Irish playwright. Quentin and I used to call him 'the Indian Hermit', though self-denial was not his strong point as he always drank too much alcohol: one late evening falling over in Upper Street, rebounding from a tailor's shop window and rolling across the pavement. Anyway, it was in such company I first met Dannie Abse. After which, we would meet up periodically for lunch in a pizza restaurant in Mortimer Street next the Middlesex Hospital where Dannie was then a radiographer.

As mentioned above, when Patricia decided to publish a literary magazine (*Acumen Literary Journal* in 1985), I took her to meet him in the pizza restaurant. Immediately, Dannie became enthusiastic over the prospect of a new poetry journal and promptly became, as Patricia has told, its first subscriber with a £5 note. Then, the meal ended, he took us to his house at Golders Green where we met Joan Abse for the first time. After which Dannie ushered us into his book-lined study in the ground floor front room facing the very suburban street called Hodford Road. There he offered items of both poetry and prose for possible use in the first issue of *Acumen* whenever it appeared. It had been over our meal in Central London that Patricia had expressed her fear that she would not be able to find enough material to make up her magazine. But this was something that Dannie, and myself, assured her could be easily overcome. And Dannie and I and many others contributed work to the first published issue of *Acumen*.

The next significant encounter was with Dannie and Joan (it was destined almost always thereafter we would be a foursome); and it came about through another decision Patricia made.

After she had left school, Patricia had become a science graduate in analytical chemistry. But after she started her literary magazine, she felt she should become a mature student in English literature at some university. Having secured a place at Westfield College – later merged with Queen Mary's University, London – whose campus was in West Hampstead, situated about a half-hour's walk from the Abses' house, we saw a great deal of them from then onwards.

As with Sebastian, so with Dannie, our relationship became in David Perman's memorable phrase a case of 'poetry and friendship'. Poetic intimacy was most marked when Dannie and I consulted each other over poems of each other's. Many a time we spent in his study, or in the large backroom-cum-conservatory of the house, going over a new poem of his or mine. The talk always of 'cliché', 'rhythm', 'metaphor', 'handling of syntax', 'meaning', etc. He was always marginally better than myself about changing a word.

Then there were poetry readings – sometimes given jointly as on one memorable occasion in the City's Barbican Library. Then at the more down-market but ever-memorable readings at the Torriano Meeting House. Most frequent were the occasions when Dannie and I attended each other's readings. The very last of which he did this year, when he came to King's College in the Strand for the launch of my *Collected and New Poems*, and remained with us for almost the entire evening. Though 91 years old, there was no sign that evening of any decline in my friend. Sadly, however, four months later Dannie died. In the last phone call between us, when he knew he had incurable cancer, he said: 'I'm ready to go, William.' But none of the rest of us were ready for his departure. But leave us he did: another loss of this Year of Losses. Another change in this Year of Changes. But one knows in one's heart things do get better. And they have: the pieces do get picked up...eventually.

27.
AFTERWORD

One small note of wisdom: this is a good life. We – humankind – alone make it bad.

First, let us consider the State of Poetry. An unhappy country and a confusing one. Unhappy because my many years involvement has shown a number of seemingly insuperable difficulties connected with it. Above all the problem of obtaining a *just critical evaluation of contemporary poetry*. In regard to most areas of supposed worth my father used to say: it's not what you know, but who you know. Of equal relevance to this difficulty of recognising – and of gaining just recognition for – the quality of poetry, published or otherwise, one should always recall Ben Jonson's view of contemporary Elizabethan and Jacobean work – that which we lump together as Tudor – it was of poor quality, he felt, compared to the products of the Classical world. Whereas, of course, posterity takes the view that Tudor poetry and theatre represent the greatest period, in terms of quality, in English literary history, and surpassing in terms of poetry most other historical eras in any land.

In my time several attempts have been made to devise ways of arriving at correct assessments of 'the best' in contemporary poetry. Systems of awards, prizes, admissions into fashionable anthologies, etc. have all been tried. Likewise, and because of the media dominance as a supposed measure of 'the truth', publishers and impresarios of poetry have combined to choose a limited number of poets to be the official representatives of quality. Example, an arbitrarily-chosen group of poets as being representative of their generation for, say, the ten years following. And while in all things a certain gesture has to be made towards democracy, none of the organisations whose job it is to 'assess the best' has a staff any way near large enough to meticulously examine *all* the books of poetry produced in this country alone in a given period, and thus arrive at a truer assessment of the best. In short: volume defeats intention. Something, for example, that is clearly noticeable each time the poets chosen, by whatever exercise is carried out, are those published by the same six or seven presses.

Finally, two other critical 'problems' deserving of mention. For all the time I have been involved with poetry, the question of endorsement by editors of poetry journals prior to the publication of a collection has been important, even crucial, to many publishers' editors and reviewers. Put simply, if a poetry collection cannot acknowledge a reasonably impressive list of appearances in magazines or in other media, say broadcasting or competition winning, then the book is sure to go un-reviewed. A clear proof of the fact that poems are not regarded as sufficient alone to 'speak for themselves'. This fact was first drawn to my attention years ago by Robert Graves who refused to preface his Collected Poems with a list of such endorsements; though it did not guarantee him the neglect it would most poets, as he was already institutionally approved as one of the poets of World War One..

The other 'difficulty' which has arisen during my time has come about as a consequence of the rise of the creative writing industry. Much has been written about the advantages and disadvantages of 'workshopping' poems before seeking their publication, so I will raise here the only negative aspect that I think important. And that is, like anything produced in committee, a workshopped poem tends towards a safe compromise and bland end-product. As in life, so in poetry, things tend towards middle-of-the-road or 'mainstream'. Which, of course, partly accounts for that portion of the poetry world which, since approximately the beginning of the 1960's, has lurched (like all the arts?) into the deliberately inchoate and pointlessly experimental.

Poetry's critical problems apart, Patricia's and my involvement in what I now think of as the administrative side of poetry has been considerable. In an earlier chapter I discussed something of the annual Torbay Poetry Festival. As I write the festival has just completed its sixteenth year and, as long as Patricia and I have the interest and energy it will continue. The same can be said for *Acumen* magazine and its publishing arm Acumen Publications. Especially with the festival though we know, through meeting hopefully all attendees, that it gives great pleasure and has developed a friendly atmosphere: 'One long poetry party' as the late Martin Blythe put it. And though one knows that poets, whose work may have been rejected by Patricia for the magazine, will get no pleasure from that particular experience, many readers and poets nevertheless do enjoy the regular appearance of the journal. The longevity of such ventures, of course, not only depends on the organizers' efforts, but one should never forget those two other difficult associates: Finance and Cost. Then there are the all-important volunteers. For much of the life of the Torbay Poetry Festival Patricia and I have been sustained by John and Suzy Miles, both theatrical people and poets. Next Danny Pyle and Brenda Hutchings. Danny, an ex-RAF man with a gift for what is called 'light verse'; and Brenda a portrait painter who, like John and Suzy, is also a thespian: one who appears regularly in plays and, also, at comedy 'gigs'. With the occasional help from others like the late-lamented David Beugger, these few individuals have made such considerable contributions to the running of the Festival that, without them, it could not have lasted for so long.

Lastly, and most especially, when writing about people and characters whom one has known, or observed, one has to try, as far as possible, not to give offence, whilst still remaining as accurate and truthful as possible. This I have tried to do. But, in one or two instances, written chapters have been removed at the request of interested parties. Consequently, this report from The Mount is not entirely complete; but the reader can be assured it is not misleading.